Y

FORTRESS • 82

SCOTTISH BARONIAL CASTLES 1250–1450

MICHAEL BROWN

ILLUSTRATED BY ADAM HOOK

Series editors Marcus Cowper and Nikolai Bogdanovic

First published in Great Britain in 2009 by Osprey Publishing
Midland House, West Way, Botley, Oxford OX2 0PH, UK
443 Park Avenue South, New York, NY 10016, USA
E-mail: info@ospreypublishing.com

ISBN: 978-1-84603-286-8
E-book ISBN: 978-1-84603-872-3

Editorial by Ilios Publishing, Oxford, UK (www.iliospublishing.com)
Page layout by Ken Vail Graphic Design, Cambridge, UK (kvgd.com)
Typeset in Sabon and Myriad Pro
Cartography: Bounford.com
Index by Margaret Vaudrey
Originated by United Graphic Pte Ltd, Singapore
Printed in China through Bookbuilders

09 10 11 12 13   10 9 8 7 6 5 4 3 2 1

A CIP catalogue record for this book is available from the British Library.

For a catalogue of all books published by Osprey Military and Aviation please contact:

NORTH AMERICA
Osprey Direct, c/o Random House Distribution Center, 400 Hahn Road, Westminster, MD 21157, USA
Email: info@ospreydirect.com

ALL OTHER REGIONS
Osprey Direct, The Book Service Ltd, Distribution Centre, Colchester Road, Frating Green, Colchester, Essex, CO7 7DW, UK
E-mail: customerservice@ospreypublishing.com

www.ospreypublishing.com

DEDICATION

For Robert and Isabelle.

ACKNOWLEDGEMENTS AND IMAGE CREDITS

Thanks are due to Undiscovered Scotland (www.undiscoveredscotland.co.uk) for permission to use the images that appear on their excellent website, and to John Richards for creating the four mono line drawing illustrations.

Unless otherwise credited all photographs and drawings are from the author's collection.

ARTIST'S NOTE

Readers may care to note that the original paintings from which the colour artwork plates in this book were prepared are available for private sale. All reproduction copyright whatsoever is retained by the Publishers. All enquiries should be addressed to:

Scorpio Gallery, PO Box 475, Hailsham, East Sussex BN27 2SL, UK

The Publishers regret that they can enter into no correspondence upon this matter.

THE FORTRESS STUDY GROUP (FSG)

The object of the FSG is to advance the education of the public in the study of all aspects of fortifications and their armaments, especially works constructed to mount or resist artillery. The FSG holds an annual conference in September over a long weekend with visits and evening lectures, an annual tour abroad lasting about eight days, and an annual Members' Day.

The FSG journal *FORT* is published annually, and its newsletter *Casemate* is published three times a year. Membership is international. For further details, please contact:

The Secretary, c/o 6 Lanark Place, London W9 1BS, UK

Website: www.fsgfort.com

THE WOODLAND TRUST

Osprey Publishing are supporting the Woodland Trust, the UK's leading woodland conservation charity, by funding the dedication of trees.

CONTENTS

SCOTTISH BARONIAL CASTLES 1250–1450

INTRODUCTION

Along with the ruined shells of the great abbeys, Scotland's castles provide the most impressive symbols of the country's medieval past. The best known, and most visited, of these are Edinburgh and Stirling castles. Perched on their rocky crags, these sites have centuries-long associations with the Scottish crown as royal fortresses and residences, but little survives of either of the medieval castles at their heart. As they appear today, Edinburgh and Stirling are essentially palaces of the Renaissance, modified after 1650 into military barracks. Instead, the true medieval castles in Scotland can be found amongst those buildings constructed by the nobility. The most memorable of these are the stone castles constructed between 1250 and 1450, which, though largely ruined, capture the sense of Scotland in the Middle Ages.

For centuries, these nobles have been criticized as robber barons, disobedient to their kings, at feud with their neighbours and backward in their tastes and instincts. The castles of such men were looked on as strongholds in a violent world, built with considerations of defence absolutely paramount. But baronial castles were more than just lairs for violent thugs. As buildings they present a picture of the nobility that is more varied, complex and sophisticated. Each castle represents different needs and concerns, balancing requirements of security, of residence and of government. The period between 1250 and 1450 represents the high point of Scottish castle-building. These two centuries witnessed the construction of many of the best-known and most important castles in the kingdom. They were the residences of famous, and infamous, aristocratic families, great baronial houses like the Black and Red Douglases, the Stewarts, the Murrays and the Comyns. All were built to provide settings for these great lords and their retinues, as centres for the running of their estates and to display their wealth and power as great men, as magnates. However, all would also experience war in the conflicts with England or in the internal clashes that disturbed the politics of the kingdom.

The story of these castles is bound up with the story of medieval Scotland. The earliest use of the word castle in the years around 1100 can be associated with the arrival and influence of Norman lords in Scotland. Though, unlike the rest of the British Isles, the Normans came and settled in Scotland as vassals of the native line of kings, their presence altered the character of the kingdom. The castle was part of this contribution. Many of these early structures were of the motte and bailey type found elsewhere, but older styles were also used. Earth banks and wooden palisades were constructed to fortify cliff-top promontaries, as at Cruggleton in Galloway, or rocky craigs, like Edinburgh and Stirling. Such sites often had long histories as refuges or fortified power centres and were simply being adapted in accordance with current tastes.

It was only with the construction of the first major stone castles in the 13th century that Scotland's castles can be analyzed with any confidence. For much of southern and eastern Scotland the years between 1220 and 1286, when these castles were built, marked a period of relative peace and prosperity under the rule of kings Alexander II and III. In this era the earls and barons of the kingdom were united in their sense of loyalty to the crown and operated in a stable environment both within Scotland and in its dealings with England. Though the western seaboard and Isles represented a more robust frontier region, it is not surprising that later generations saw these years as a 'golden age'.

The 'golden age' ended abruptly in 1286. The death of Alexander III brought to an end the line of Scottish kings that had presided over the kingdom's development into a European-style realm since 1100. Tensions over the succession began to build and were exploited by the masterful English king, Edward I, who enforced his claim to sovereignty over Scotland. When the new Scottish king, John Balliol, tried to resist, Edward I led an army north, ending the long peace between England and Scotland. In a few weeks in early 1296 Edward overran Scotland, but this conquest proved to be an illusion. Instead the war that began in 1296 lasted for decades. Scotland's castles became the keys to the kingdom, crucial military bases and objectives for rival armies and factions. Despite the greater resources of the English kings, it would be Robert Bruce and his heirs as leaders of an independent Scottish community who would gain control of Scotland and her castles, leaving most of them in ruins.

The period of major warfare with England ended in the 1350s. Politically and architecturally, the following century was one of reconstruction and recovery from these intense conflicts. The winners of the struggle were not just the Bruce kings but those nobles who had supported them, above all the Stewarts and Douglases. Lords from these families acquired new lands and greater status as the magnates of the realm. Their resources in rents and in men even rivalled that of the crown (which passed to the house of Stewart

Coulter Motte is a typical small motte of the 12th century. It shows the difficulty of understanding noble residences in Scotland before 1200.

in 1371). The greatest castles of this period were built by Stewart and Douglas magnates as places of strength and to display their power. Smaller castles followed similar approaches and reflected the ambitions of the large group of middle- and lesser-ranking nobles. By the mid-15th century the quest for increased authority and wealth by the Stewart kings, James I and James II, and the support they won from within the noble class would bring down the greatest magnate houses, those of Albany and Black Douglas. The end of these families brought a new era in Scottish castle-building.

CHRONOLOGY

1214-49	Reign of Alexander II.
c. **1220**	Maxwells acquire Caerlaverock. Construction of the first castle.
1230	Norwegians take Rothesay Castle.
c. **1240–60**	Construction of Dirleton Castle.
c. **1240–80**	Construction of Kildrummy Castle.
1249–86	Reign of Alexander III.
1263	Norse fleet in the Firth of Clyde. Battle of Largs.
c. **1270**	Construction of the second castle at Caerlaverock
c. **1260-80**	Construction of the donjon at Bothwell
1296	Edward I overruns Scotland. Onset of war with England.

The main surviving buildings of Edinburgh Castle, the most famous in Scotland, date from after 1500. Only its chapel and site remain from the great royal fortress residence of the Middle Ages.

The locations of the castles mentioned in this book

N

NORTH SEA

Balvenie
Huntly
Tolquhoun
Lochindorb
Urquhart
Kildrummy
Ruthven
Lumphanan
Coull
Strachan
Inverlochy
Blair
Tioram
Mingary
Moulin
SCOTLAND
Dunstaffnage
Kinclaven
St Andrews
Doune
Lochleven
Aberdour
Stirling
Rosyth
Tantallon
Sween
Blackness
Dirleton
Abercorn
Dunoon
Dundas
Crichton
Skipness
Rothesay
Bothwell
Craigmillar
Borthwick
Lochranza
Neidpath
Smailholm
Brodick
Newark
Dundonald
Cessford
Hermitage
Lochmaben
ENGLAND
Caerlaverock
NORTHERN
IRELAND
Threave
Cruggleton

0   30 miles
0   50km

7

The site of Clunie Castle in Perthshire gives an indication of the small scale and limited complexity of many royal castles still used in the 13th century. A stepped, artificial mound topped with a small stone hall was the basis of this fortification.

1297	Uprising led by William Wallace and Andrew Murray.
1299	Scots force Stirling Castle to surrender after blockade.
1300	The siege of Caerlaverock. Captured by Edward I.
1301	Edward I captures Bothwell Castle.
1304	Siege of Stirling Castle. Its fall ends Scottish resistance to Edward I.
1306	Robert Bruce seizes throne, and captures number of small castles. Kildrummy Castle captured by Prince Edward of England.
1312–13	Bruce's partisans capture Dundee, Buittle, Caerlaverock and Perth.
1314	James Douglas takes Roxburgh and Thomas Randolph captures Edinburgh. Siege of Stirling and battle of Bannockburn.
1318	Capture of Berwick Castle and town.
1328	Peace between Robert I King of Scots and Edward III of England.
1333	Edward III renews war against Scotland. English capture Berwick.
1335–36	Refortification of castles by Edward III.
1337	Andrew Murray captures Bothwell, Kinclaven and St Andrews.
1346	David II defeated at Neville's Cross. Fall of Caerlaverock, Lochmaben and Roxburgh to English.
1357	Truce of Berwick ends period of major Anglo-Scottish warfare.
c. 1350s	Construction of Tantallon Castle by William lord of Douglas (from 1358, first earl of Douglas).
c. 1362	Refortification of Bothwell by Archibald Douglas 'the Grim'.
c. 1360–80s	Construction of Doune Castle by Robert Stewart earl of Fife and Menteith.
1371	Accession of Robert II as first Stewart King of Scots.
c. 1370s	Construction of Threave Castle by Archibald Douglas.

c. 1400s–20s	Reconstruction of Bothwell and Caerlaverock.
1425	James I has the Duke of Albany executed. Doune and Falkland pass to the crown.
1450–55	Conflicts between James II and the Black Douglases end with exile of family. Threave, Bothwell and Newark pass to the crown.

13TH-CENTURY CASTLES

Castles and their builders

13th-century Scotland witnessed the construction of a small group of finely built and well-defended noble houses. Castles like Kildrummy in Aberdeenshire, Dirleton in Lothian, Bothwell in Clydesdale and Caerlaverock near Dumfries were built in stone with high, round towers, a great residential tower or donjon and strongly defended gates. They have often been seen as representing a high point in castle design and construction in medieval Scotland. They were not the earliest stone castles in the northern British Isles. Even before 1200 stone was being used in fortifications in the west, in Argyll and the Hebrides. However, castles like Sween, Tioram and Mingary were built on rocky headlands by sea lords of mixed Scandinavian and Gaelic blood. They belonged to a different tradition and environment to eastern and southern Scotland and were not the models for buildings in these regions. Nor were the great castles typical of the houses of nobles in the 13th century. Many of the earth and timber castles constructed before 1200 continued to be used, though some, like Cruggleton and Buittle in Galloway and Cupar in Fife, had their timber palisades replaced with stone walls. There is archaeological evidence from sites like the Pele of Lumphanan and Castlehill of Strachan that nobles continued to build motte and bailey castles in the 13th century, though it has been suggested that these provided secondary residences, such as hunting lodges. The centre of such constructions would have been a hall of wood or stone, and for many lords a free-standing hall house without a walled enclosure would have been sufficient lodging.

Whether a Scottish noble chose to build a castle and the type of castle he constructed or resided in depended on a range of factors. The scale of a building did not necessarily denote the status or even the wealth of its owner.

The Murrays clearly meant to build a larger castle at Bothwell. The precise plan is obscured by the later construction at the castle, but the foundations of two gate towers have been unearthed north of the donjon. These suggest that an extensive circuit of walls was envisaged, protected by a gatehouse similar to that at Caerlaverock and Kildrummy.

The donjon or great tower at Bothwell Castle, and the small section of wall to the left, are the only parts of the structure completed before 1300. The entrance to the tower is through the well-guarded door at ground level (partly obscured by scaffolding).

The limited evidence of the royal castles of the 13th-century kings does not suggest that they were the strongest or most sophisticated structures in the land. Though Edinburgh, Stirling and Roxburgh were places of great natural strength and were well fortified, they lacked the full range of features found in some private castles. Other royal castles, like Kinclaven and Clunie, were much smaller and simpler though still in use. The same point can be made about the castles of the greatest nobles, the earls and provincial lords. Scotland's senior noble family, the earls of Fife, possessed a small castle at Cupar and resided elsewhere in halls like those known to have stood at Rathillet and Rires in their earldom. The earls of Menteith, Strathearn and Lennox similarly showed little interest in constructing major castles. Though the southern earls of Dunbar had a strategically important and naturally strong castle on the coast at Dunbar, the construction of a large and impressive castle at Kildrummy by the earls of Mar was the exception rather than the rule amongst the dozen or so Scottish earls. Similarly amongst the greatest barons, the Bruces, Balliols and Durwards were content with relatively small or simple residences. The Bruces probably replaced the motte and bailey castle at Lochmaben with a simple stone castle nearby as their main centre in Annandale, while the Balliols, who inherited the chief share of Galloway in 1234, simply strengthened the existing castle at Buittle. The choices of these magnates do not reflect a lack of resources. The earls of Fife, the Balliols and the Bruces all possessed sizeable landed incomes drawn from estates in Scotland and in England.

A THE CASTLE IN THE WEST – INVERLOCHY AND THE ATTACK OF THE ISLESMEN IN 1297

In 1297 the Comyns' garrison at Inverlochy Castle was attacked by a force from the Western Isles. The attackers arrived by boat up Loch Linnhe and, after a fight on the shore, burned the galleys drawn up under the castle walls. Two of these were said to be the largest in the Isles. However, the castle was too strong for this force to capture, and the Islesmen withdrew. Inverlochy is seen from the north, flying the Comyns' standard, with Ben Nevis behind it.

A

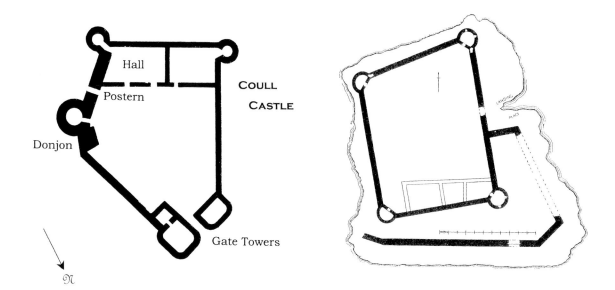

Hall

Postern

Donjon

COULL
CASTLE

Gate Towers

N

Nobles of wealth and importance chose to reside at the traditional centres of their lands. Though they might fortify and enlarge older residences, their choices reflected a desire to maintain the continuity of their family's influence and powers. Where new castles were built this can similarly be explained by the concerns of noble owners as landlords and figures of status. These concerns included needs of defence and warfare. In the north and west of Scotland, in provinces like Moray, Lochaber and Argyll, the crown and its supporters had faced repeated opposition from local kindreds. As in Wales and Ireland, in these regions the castles built by the kings and by nobles were instruments of control, both political and military. The clearest examples of this are provided by the Stewarts in the west and the Comyns in the north. Around the Firth of Clyde, by 1286 Stewart magnates had built or taken over castles at Inverkip and Dundonald on the mainland, Rothesay on Bute, Dunoon in Argyll, Lochranza and Brodick on Arran and Skipness and Sween in Knapdale and Kintyre. These formed a network of strongpoints from which the Stewarts extended and maintained their influence in a region that was a frontier between the Scottish realm and the powerful rulers of the Isles who, up to 1266, were subjects of the King of Norway. When Norse fleets were sent to the Isles in 1230 and 1263 to strengthen Norwegian influence in the west, they directed their attacks against the Stewarts and their castles. Though Rothesay fell in 1230, the castles served their lords well.

Similar motives lay behind the construction of castles by the Comyn family in their Highland lordship of Badenoch and Lochaber. Between 1230 and 1280 they constructed residences at Lochindorb, Ruthven and Inverlochy, whose sites suggest strategic concerns. In the Highlands, accessible routes were few in number and important to control. Ruthven was built at the southern end of the Spey Valley near the passes to the south while Lochindorb stood at the northern edge of the Comyn lordship on the edge of the Moray lowlands. Inverlochy was probably the last of these castles to be built and the most important. It lay at the head of Loch Linnhe and the foot of the Great Glen and was intended both as a base to police the western Isles and coastlands and to command access to Moray from the west. Another castle at Urquhart, held by Alan Durward, confirmed the importance of the glen in the management of the Highlands.

However, the most impressive 13th-century castles were not built in these marcher lordships but in lands of peace. Dirleton and Bothwell lay in the relatively stable heartlands of the kingdom and, while Caerlaverock stood near the borders of both Galloway and England, sources of possible trouble, it is unlikely that it was built to guard against physical threats. Kildrummy was a northern castle and lay near the routes into Moray, but by the time it was built the need to defend these roads hardly required the scale of the building. In all four examples the reasons for construction related less to fears about security than to more peaceful concerns. The nobles who built Dirleton, Caerlaverock and Bothwell were not earls or great magnates. Bothwell was the work of William Murray, Dirleton was built by John Vaux and Caerlaverock by Aymer or Herbert Maxwell. All of these were barons of middle rank, influential and wealthy as Murray's nickname '*le Riche*' indicates. Their families had risen in the king's service. Such men probably built their castles on a scale designed to display their wealth and aspirations. Magnificent residences would lift them above neighbouring nobles and, for the Murrays and Maxwells who built in estates they had only recently acquired, establish their families in local society. The reasons for Kildrummy's construction were similar. The earls of Mar did not need a new residence. They already possessed castles in their earldom but chose to divert considerable resources into the building of a new stronghold. Like the nobles named above, Earl William of Mar built to confirm his status. His decision may have been influenced by the rival claims of Alan Durward to the earldom of Mar. Durward also possessed a stone castle at Coull and Earl William perhaps constructed Kildrummy to symbolize his pre-eminence in the north-east. Similar motives led to the Comyns constructing a castle at Blair in Atholl designed to rival the *Caisteal Dubh* (Black Castle) of Earl David of Atholl at Moulin near Pitlochry. In these cases, building was a means of competition, asserting local leadership through a castle that was physically imposing; it also acted as a centre of entertainment and private justice and, if needed, a secure base for feud or warfare.

Kinclaven Castle has a simple square plan without gatehouse. It may have had corner towers, but these did not project above the walls and may have been added in the 14th century.

The gatehouse with round towers flanking the entrance was developed at Caerlaverock and Dirleton as a defensive feature and as a residence. As well as covering the entrance and providing lines of defence, the lord's chamber and halls at both castles were located in or adjacent to the round towers.

This illustration shows the main entrances at these castles as they would have been in the 13th century. Caerlaverock is shown from the north-west (1) showing the Lord's Chamber and hall in cutaway detail, while Dirleton is shown from the south-east (2), with a cutaway of the Lord's Hall.

Castle design and function

All castles were unique. As discussed previously, they were constructed and adapted to meet the needs and resources of their owners. They were also tailored to their immediate site and the wider landscape. For some lords it was enough to develop existing castles previously protected by earthworks and timber palisades. An example of this process which reveals much about building techniques has been found at Cruggleton in Galloway. This site on a cliff-top promontory overlooking Wigtown Bay had been a noble residence since the 8th century and had been fortified in the late 12th century with an earth mound or motte topped by a palisade. In about 1290 its lord, John Comyn earl of Buchan, had Cruggleton strengthened. A stone wall was built around the foot of the motte, resting on a foundation of clay and boulders. This wall was probably less than two metres high and backed onto the motte. The entrance was in the north wall and a stone tower or hall house was built on the summit along with other timber buildings. The result was probably a castle which was only slightly stronger in terms of defence but which was much more physically impressive than its predecessor.

Dirleton Castle, showing the main entrance and great tower. Though less impressive than the donjon at Bothwell, this drum tower contained the lord's lodging and hall in the 13th-century castle. A second tower flanked the gateway on the other side, but this was destroyed in the wars after 1296.

The interior of the lord's hall at Dirleton. While relatively small and dark to a modern eye, the polygonal chamber was well designed with rib vaulting and window seats and would have provided a warm and comfortable home for the lord and his family.

Even when new castles were constructed in the 13th century the level of sophistication varied considerably. The castles built before 1250 at Rothesay, Balvenie and Kinclaven were essentially simple walled enclosures. In their original form all three castles seem to have lacked large towers and internal stone buildings. They relied for defence on the height of their walls, which could be defended by men on the wall walk running inside the battlements. At Rothesay the early wall head is preserved in the later, higher wall showing the narrow gaps left for archery between the protective blocks (merlons). While Balvenie and Kinclaven are square in shape, Rothesay was roughly circular, but the lack of projecting towers was a weakness for all three. In 1230 Rothesay was besieged by a fleet from Norway and the Isles. The archery of the defenders on the ramparts failed to prevent the Norse undermining the wall at a weak point and taking the castle. When the Stewarts rebuilt their stronghold they added four round towers spaced at regular intervals. These would allow the garrison to command the base of the walls more effectively, preventing a repeat of the attack of 1230.

Round towers became a feature of almost all Scottish castles built in the decades after 1250. The best examples from the period all reflect common elements of design. They are enclosed by a curtain wall of irregular or roughly square or triangular shape, which was strengthened at the angles by the construction of round towers of varying heights and diameter. The castle of Lochindorb built on an island in a loch by the Comyns represents the most simple form of this. The towers are small relative to the length of wall they defend and seem to have stood only two storeys high. Moreover the towers only projected slightly from the walls, making them easier to construct but less valuable for defence. Other northern castles showed a greater degree of sophistication. At Coull in Aberdeenshire a small irregular enclosure had three or possibly four towers at its corners, while at their important castle of Inverlochy the Comyns constructed a castle of roughly square shape, about 30 metres by 40 metres in size. Its walls were 10 metres high and three metres thick and it had simple gateways in the north and south walls. Inverlochy's principal strength was in the four projecting round or drum towers at the corners. These both provided lodging for the men of the castle and commanded the approach to the castle. They also protected access to the walls should an enemy enter the courtyard. Three of the towers were of a similar size, but the fourth, later called the Comyn Tower, was larger in girth and possibly higher. It is believed that this was a great tower or donjon, the centre of the castle. This applied both to its defensive strength and to the more spacious apartments it contained, designed as accommodation for the lord, or, more normally, for his steward of Lochaber to hold his court.

The form and role of the great tower is illustrated most impressively by Bothwell Castle. Here the Murrays built a magnificent donjon out of finely cut blocks of red sandstone. It is 20 metres in diameter and, though ruined, stands over 27 metres high. The donjon stood within its own moat, which could be crossed by a drawbridge, features suggesting an intention to make the tower a defensible strongpoint. This massive building may have been designed as the defensive heart of a large castle, but its design reveals other priorities. The tower was built to impress. Access was through a single arched doorway into a high, vaulted hall, lit by fine, gothic windows set into recesses. This was presumably intended to be the outer part of the lord's apartments where tenants and servants would have met with their master. Above were two other chambers, each large and well appointed. The top level, with its double windows, was probably the chamber of lord and lady, not a wholly private space but the inner core of the residence, where the Murrays met with their intimate advisers and friends and could entertain noble, even royal, visitors.

This great tower was only the centre of the spectacular castle planned by William Murray. Unearthed foundations reveal that work was begun on a much larger castle with at least three other angle towers and a double-towered gatehouse. Of this only the donjon, one small tower and a short section of curtain wall were built before work was halted, probably by the onset of war in 1296. Murray's plans reveal a desire to include features being incorporated into other contemporary castles. The most interesting new feature is the towered gatehouse. The best example of this is found at Caerlaverock. Here the Maxwells made the gatehouse the focus of the castle they built in the 1270s. The whole plan is highly distinctive. Abandoning an earlier simple stone castle in the marsh to the south, the Maxwells constructed a triangular enclosure within two moats. Described in 1300 as 'shaped like a shield', the apex of the triangle was the castle entrance. The gate was guarded by a double tower, built, like Bothwell, of high-quality stone blocks. This was intended to provide a strong defence at the weakest point in the circuit of walls, but also functioned as the lord's residence. Though later damage and reconstruction make analysis of Caerlaverock problematic, the top floors of the gate towers probably housed the chambers, as at Bothwell. Behind the towers was a further block in which a stone-vaulted hall provided additional space for the lord and his servants. This complex of rooms was both a gate defence and donjon, but its purpose seems less explicable in terms of security than of taste and comfort. The layout of Caerlaverock created a distinctive and strikingly regular castle residence whose site, in a dip of ground, may have been chosen to provide an elegant view of the gatehouse flanked by the rear towers. Defensible it certainly was, but Caerlaverock was also designed to impress.

Similar concerns were behind the design of Dirleton Castle. It was built on an outcrop of rock in the rich fields of Lothian, east of Edinburgh. Here, too, drum towers both served as defensive features and formed the focus of the building as the centre of a baronial household and visual representation of status. Rather than a gatehouse, at Dirleton towers flanked the entrance at a distance. More importantly the grouping of towers in the southern corner of the castle created a complex of rooms that provided its domestic heart. The great tower housed kitchens at ground level with a fine, almost intimate hexagonal hall over them. Ancillary rooms, such as the chapel and a withdrawing room, were contained in flanking smaller towers, while the great hall of the castle, where ordinary servants dined and where the lord could hold large gatherings, was a timber structure in the castle yard abutting the towers.

The great 13th-century castle of Couci-le-Château, showing one of the numerous drum towers. The use of round towers, its triangular plan and its towering donjon (destroyed in World War I) have led many to link its design to contemporary Scottish castles. Its lords had marriage ties to the Scottish royal house.

While a castle like Dirleton was much more than a fortress, security was a consideration. In 1242 a violent feud with the Comyns forced Hugh Bisset to shelter behind the walls of his castle at Aboyne in Aberdeenshire. However, there was no siege, just the standard harrying of lands and livestock. A much cheaper and less developed house than the castles at Kildrummy, Dirleton or even Coull would have sufficed. What builders sought was an impression of power and status which had a strong, military character – defensible residences that provided relative luxury for their owners.

The construction of Dirleton, Bothwell, Caerlaverock and their ilk put the castle-builders and owners of Scotland on a par with those of other lands. Castles from elsewhere provide interesting parallels and, perhaps, models for the most striking Scottish castles. The most intriguing model is that of the great château of Couci in north-east France. Alexander II's second queen, Marie, was from the great noble house of Couci and the negotiation of this match in the late 1230s may have taken servants of the Scottish king to Couci, where the lord had just completed a massive castle. This had an irregular four-sided plan with the angles guarded by great drum towers. The heart of the building was an immense donjon more than 65 metres high separated from the courtyard by its own ditch and abutting a stone great hall. The design has strong similarities with Bothwell's donjon, the layout of Kildrummy and the use of towers at Dirleton, whose lord, John Vaux was said to have been Queen Marie's steward. It might be expected that, closer to home, the numerous ties of family, land and friendship between Scottish nobles and the vassals of the English king in the 13th century would influence castle-building in Scotland. However the largest castles of northern England, like Middleham, Richmond and Brougham, seem quite different with square donjons and mural towers. Yet comparisons with Scottish styles can be found. The castle of Beeston in Cheshire is one of the earliest in the British Isles to include a gatehouse with drum towers. It was built in the 1220s by the earl of Chester, a noble with strong Scottish connections. In the great marcher lordships of Wales too, round towers and curtain walls were employed. At Kidwelly, for example, the design bears close comparison with that of Inverlochy, while the huge fortress constructed by the earls of Gloucester at Caerphilly in the 1270s employs two

One of the earliest examples of the round-towered gatehouse in the British Isles is at Beeston Castle in Cheshire. It was built by the earls of Chester in the 1220s.

great fortified gatehouses. These foreshadow those built by Edward I's masons at his great Welsh castles like Harlech, Conway and Beaumaris in the 1280s and 1290s to cement his conquest of the princes of Wales. Though direct links have been drawn between the Edwardian castles and baronial structures in Scotland, the timing makes this unlikely. Limited work would be done by Edward's builders in Scotland, but the use of round-towered gatehouses at Caerlaverock and Kildrummy may have reflected less specific awareness of the value of these features. Scotland's baronial castles were an up-to-date expression of taste and resources built by barons aware of European models of noble architecture.

TOUR OF A SITE – KILDRUMMY CASTLE

Kildrummy is a magnificent wreck of a castle. All but one of its towers are broken stumps, its gatehouse is levelled and the hall and chapel within its courtyard survive only as bare, ruined walls. Despite this, Kildrummy remains a model of baronial castle-building in the years before 1300. Its ruins convey the aims and tastes of both its builders and its lords and the main features of the greatest 13th-century residences of Scottish noblemen.

The castle stands among the rolling hills of western Mar on the fringes of the Grampians. It was built on rising ground and commands two natural route ways. The first runs along the nearby River Don, which flowed west from the mountains to the sea at Aberdeen. The second passes through the low hills south to the valley of the Dee and north to Strathbogie and the Moray Firth. This location had value in terms of the castle's military role but, more routinely, made it a natural centre from which the earls of Mar could run their estates in the districts between the Dee and the Don. Kildrummy was the caput, the head place, of Mar from the late 13th to 15th centuries, where the earls held their courts, settling local disputes, and meeting with and entertaining their vassals and neighbours. To support the earls and their households, by the 15th century there was a settlement, a castle toun, outside the walls that would house both servants and their families and craftsmen who could supply the castle community with its needs. As the ground north of the castle falls away steeply to a burn, the houses and workshops must have stood before the castle gate and the ditch which covered the approach from the lower ground to the south.

Kildrummy Castle from the east. The damage to the site is obvious, but so too is its impressive setting and the scale of the fortifications and accommodation built and inhabited by the earls of Mar between the 13th and 17th centuries.

The castle that loomed over the low houses shared many features with the contemporary works at Bothwell and Caerlaverock. Like them, it relied for defence on its circuit of high curtain walls, protected at the vulnerable angles by round towers and at its entrance by a double-towered gatehouse. Like the planned castle of the Murrays at Bothwell too, its core, both defensive and residential, was a great round tower, at Kildrummy called the Snow Tower. Despite its ruined state, sufficient remains of all these features to allow some reconstruction of the castle in its early years before 1300.

The most tantalizing remains lie at the main entrance. Though only the foundations survive, these show that the gate was guarded by two projecting round towers about 4.5 metres in diameter. Behind each tower was a square chamber, perhaps guardrooms. The height and design of the upper floors of this gate complex is lost, but on the basis of the ground plan it has been suggested that this work was undertaken in the early 1300s on the orders of Edward I. The evidence for this is not conclusive. While the layout of the gatehouse is similar to the entrances at Harlech Castle, built by Edward's masons in north Wales during the 1280s, there are other parallels from amongst baronial strongholds in Wales, England and Ireland. In Scotland, Caerlaverock's twin-towered gatehouse is a complete example with similar elements to Kildrummy that clearly existed prior to the onset of war with England. The limited evidence and the short periods of English royal control make it more likely that the gate was the work of its Scottish lords and constructed in the second half of the 13th century.

The construction of such a gatehouse would have served two purposes. First, it would have provided a strong defence at the most vulnerable point in the circuit of walls. The projecting round towers would have allowed archers to cover all angles of approach to the castle from the open slope to the south and command any attacker's attempt to rush the gate itself. However, as at Caerlaverock, considerations of style should not be overlooked. Two tall towers would act as a focal point for views of Kildrummy for visitors climbing up from the River Don, giving a clear display of the prestige and martial power of the earls of Mar. Similar interlinked considerations can be used to trace the other elements of the castle's outer structures.

Kildrummy was a place of considerable strength. The gatehouse stood at the apex of a circuit of curtain walls which, though not a regular triangle like

The size of the great hall at Kildrummy is evident from the surviving remains. The large windows both on the courtyard side and through the curtain can also be seen.

Caerlaverock, had a similar shield-shaped outline. Rather than set square to the gatehouse, the curtain walls were angled northwards to two small towers, known in the 15th century as the 'Burges' and 'Maldis' towers (now generally termed south-west and south-east). These round towers survive to about nine metres in height and probably stood three storeys high. They have a D-shaped plan with a semi-circular projection from the walls. These projections covered the walls, at the foot and the parapet, and guarded vulnerable corners in the circuit of walls. Archers within the towers could fire through long arrow slits, one facing directly outwards, and one each covering the line of the curtain wall to north and south. The top of these towers could have been used as platforms for more archers or men with javelins.

The south-east tower, the chapel and the Warden's Tower at Kildrummy. The quality of the work, with the walls fronted by ashlar masonry filled with rubble, is apparent. The windows of the chapel, projecting outside the curtain, and of the Warden's Tower show similar concern for appearance.

From these small towers the walls run straight northwards to the two rear corners of the castle. These corners also have towers, the largest at Kildrummy. The eastern tower is known as the Warden's, while the western, the donjon, was called, from the later Middle Ages at least, the Snow Tower, or 'Snowdon'. The Warden's is the most complete of Kildrummy's towers. It had four floors. Its base was apparently a prison, above which stood a guardroom with arrow slits. The tower projects fully from the corner to command the rear and the steep gorge that lies there. However, its traditional name indicates it was also the residence of the castle's warden and, probably, other household servants of the earls. Its top two floors each have three sets of decorated double windows rather than arrow slits. Such windows, designed to light the chambers, not defend them, suggest the interior of the Warden's Tower contained accommodation like that at Dirleton.

At Kildrummy it is hard to escape the sense that the builders placed the primary emphasis on residential qualities. All the towers provided accommodation for the lord and his high-status servants and guests. The placing of the highest towers at the relatively secure north end of the castle may have been another means of creating an impression of strength for visitors entering the courtyard. Such a visitor would see, facing him, the Warden's Tower, the great seven-storey Snow Tower, the high roof of the great hall and, to the right, the impressive chapel. These formed the core of the castle. The chapel was about 12 metres long. All that remains above its foundations is its east end. This

C **FOLLOWING PAGES: KILDRUMMY CASTLE, *c.* 1291**

This shows a reconstruction of the castle as it was in the years before the outbreak of the wars, in both aerial and plan view. The gatehouse (1) was probably largely constructed before 1296. It bears comparison with the works at Caerlaverock, which certainly date from this period. The small flanking towers at angles in the curtain wall, identified as the south-east (2) and south-west towers (3), supported the defence of the wall walk.

The Warden's Tower (4) presumably housed the castle's constable. The chapel (5) and Great Hall (6) are of a size to indicate the concerns of the earls of Mar with domestic and spiritual needs. As at Bothwell, the lord chose to build a massive tower as his residence. Here it was termed the Snow Tower (7) and gave the castle its nickname of 'Snowdon'.

Plan view

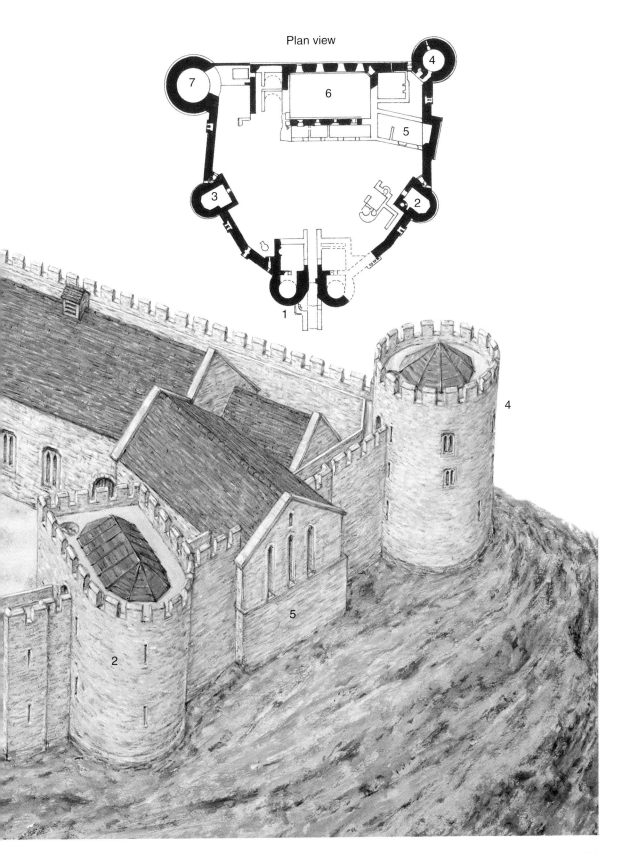

actually projected beyond the line of the curtain wall, ending in three, tall, lancet windows. These would have provided light to the interior, but hardly increased its security. The priorities of the builders are further suggested by the fact that the chapel seems to have been constructed on the foundations of an unbuilt round tower. To provide for a regular, well-lit chapel, the military strength of the castle was reduced.

Next to the chapel stood the great hall with the kitchen immediately to the east. Though it was a single-storey building, it was also designed to impress. Over 21 metres long, it was well lit with large windows on both the south side, looking onto the courtyard, and also on the north through the curtain wall. Though these stood about 3.6 metres off the ground, they provided internal light and air at the price of further weak points in Kildrummy's defence. Comfort and style were the key. The earl would have sat on a dais at the west end of the hall, which he would have entered via a covered passage.

This passage led to the Snow Tower. Though this tower collapsed in 1805, an earlier account describes it as being seven storeys high with walls up to 5.4 metres thick. As at Bothwell and Dirleton, the walls contained mural chambers and passages and in its basement was a well that provided water for the whole tower. The donjon at Bothwell seems a likely model for the Snow Tower. Like it, the Snow Tower was probably built as a donjon which could be defended if the walls had been lost. Men could mount a defence via arrow slits and from the parapet. However it is almost certain that its upper floors provided spacious and well-appointed accommodation for the earl, his family and body servants. As with contemporary and later castles, the use of a tower house as the lord's dwelling was a design influenced by questions of lordly status as much as security. The famous siege of 1306, when Kildrummy was betrayed by the treacherous blacksmith Osbern who lit a fire in the chapel and destroyed the castle's supplies, forcing its surrender to the English, was an exceptional event. The castle's longer-standing and more regular function was as a great house, built to be defended, but also designed to display the power and wealth of the earls of Mar.

THE CASTLES AT WAR, 1296–1356

The castles in the Scottish Wars

Though they were built in a period of relative peace, the castles owned by the lords of Scotland would quickly be tested in war. The end of the old line of Scottish kings aroused the ambitions of Edward I of England for power over Scotland. His efforts to exercise lordship over the new King of Scots, John Balliol, led to war in 1296. For the next 60 years this conflict boiled or simmered. Its course caught up the castles of both the crown and nobility and saw them stormed, surrendered and ruined. As the 'keys of the kingdom', they were the goals of war and the means of conquest.

Scotland's castles failed their first test in defence of the realm. Having stormed Berwick and defeated a Scottish army trying to rescue the besieged garrison of Dunbar, Edward I led his army northwards in May 1296. In less than two months, the king, lords and castles of Scotland all submitted to King Edward. Only at Edinburgh and Linlithgow was there any resistance and at the strongest royal castle, Stirling, the garrison fled leaving the porter to hand over the keys. It was a lesson that, however well constructed or naturally defensible, castles were only as strong as the men who held them, and that fear was as powerful a weapon as Edward's great siege engines.

The next year Edward was himself to learn a lesson about castles. Leaving garrisons in royal and baronial castles from Caerlaverock to Inverness and an army in Berwick, Edward turned south. These garrisons were large enough to antagonize the Scots but too small and scattered to defend themselves. Uprisings under Andrew Murray in the north and William Wallace in the south-west showed the English-held castles to be isolated and vulnerable. Beyond Berwick, Edinburgh and Roxburgh almost all fell to the Scottish leaders in 1297. It took a massive army and a bloody battle at Falkirk in 1298 before Edward could recover even some of these castles. What followed was a six-year war of attrition in which both sides saw control of castles as a key to military success. Edward placed troops in major royal castles and in baronial houses like Dirleton, Lochmaben and Bothwell. He also expected lords like Earl Patrick of Dunbar to defend their castles in his name. His opponents followed suit, manning Caerlaverock, Inverkip and, from 1299, Stirling and Bothwell. Such castle-troops waged local warfare but were also the targets of major campaigns. In 1299 the Scots took Stirling and Bothwell after long sieges. In 1300 Caerlaverock was the principal goal of Edward I's army and the following year he took Bothwell by storm on his march through the south. The climax of this war came in 1304. During the previous autumn and winter King Edward had brought the Scots to their knees with a march into the north. He had bypassed Stirling Castle, crossing the Forth on a bridge of boats, and returned to besiege this key fortress in May. The garrison, fighting 'for the Lion', the symbol of Scottish kingship, held out bravely, without hope of rescue. Their surrender in June marked the end of open resistance to Edward.

Edward I's hopes of final conquest were rocked by the rebellion of Robert Bruce in 1306. Bruce's first act was to secure castles in the south-west, as a base for his ambitions and as a bargaining counter in any negotiations. However, the key castles – Edinburgh, Stirling, Bothwell and others – resisted, and soon after proclaiming himself king Robert was defeated in battle and forced to flee into exile. The efforts of his brother Neil to delay pursuit by defending Kildrummy ended with the siege and capture of the castle. Neil

Rothesay Castle with its unusual circular plan was one of the bases of the Stewart family around the Firth of Clyde. (Undiscovered Scotland)

was brutally executed. His brother's fate may have confirmed Bruce in his view that castles served the English better than the Scots. While Edward's men needed castles as the basis for their king's rule in Scotland, the sieges of Caerlaverock, Bothwell, Stirling and Kildrummy showed that efforts to defend castles drew the Scots into the kind of warfare in which their enemy excelled. Instead, when Bruce returned to Scotland in 1307 and began to gain ground he targeted castles with the aim of destroying them. Castles remained central to his campaigns. On his march to the north in late 1307, Robert took Inverlochy by striking a deal with its garrison and Urquhart 'for want of keeping'. Over the winter, Bruce's enemies, the Comyns and their allies, defended their lands and castles against him, but in the spring Robert overran the region, putting Balvenie, Coull and other castles to the flames.

As King Robert extended his reach similar fates befell royal and baronial strongholds further south. Edward II followed his father's strategy of basing his officials and troops in a network of castles, amongst them Dunbar, Dirleton, Caerlaverock, Bothwell and Lochmaben. However, against Robert's skills his garrisons proved vulnerable. Caerlaverock fell in 1312, its owner, John Maxwell, receiving compensation for its demolition by Bruce. In 1314 Robert's captains, James Douglas and Thomas Randolph, took the key royal castles of Roxburgh and Edinburgh by surprise attacks. However, the

D EDWARD I'S SIEGE OF BOTHWELL IN SEPTEMBER 1301

To clear his way up the Clyde Valley, Edward I laid siege to the tower at Bothwell in late August and September 1301. The garrison, perhaps consisting of two knights and 32 serjeants, held out for over a month before surrendering to attacks by Edward's siege tower and engines. Archers can be seen exchanging fire with the garrison from behind archery screens on the ground, and from the top level of the siege tower. A trebuchet engine can be seen launching a missile in the lower right.

Inverlochy Castle was built by the Comyn lords of Badenoch and Lochaber probably in about 1270. Its design is relatively simple and its stonework is crude by comparison with Bothwell and Kildrummy, consisting of uncut stones, rubble and mortar. However, the use of round towers links the design with these contemporary buildings. (Undiscovered Scotland)

A map showing the location of Inverlochy Castle. Inverlochy lay on the key land and sea routes through the west and protected its own anchorage. (John Richards)

INVERLOCHY CASTLE AND ITS STRATEGIC POSITION

potential dangers posed to Robert by castles was shown at Stirling. The agreement that Stirling would surrender unless relieved by an English army gave Edward II a clear, strategic goal in a war against an elusive enemy. The English king's march to Stirling in June 1314 led Robert to risk battle at Bannockburn. For Robert the gamble paid off. Victory in battle won him Stirling and, soon after, Bothwell, whose constable surrendered after trapping several leading English nobles inside. The capture of Berwick town and castle in 1318, which followed several failed sieges, removed the last of Edward's garrisons from Scotland.

Though Robert refortified Berwick, he left other castles in the south and east in ruins to deny the English the means to rule Scotland. However, when war resumed between the kingdoms in 1333, Scottish efforts to defend Berwick resulted in a crushing battlefield defeat at Halidon Hill outside the town. There was a real danger that Edward III of England and his vassal, Edward Balliol, would reduce Scotland to a divided and subjected land. At this point, the remaining Scottish castles provided a key defence for the Bruce party. Amongst these were Dumbarton, where the young king David II took refuge, the island castle of Lochleven, which withstood a long siege in 1334, and Kildrummy. Resistance spread from these centres with leaders like Robert Stewart recovering family lands and castles, amongst them Dunoon and Rothesay. In the face of sustained resistance, in late 1335 Edward III began to refortify the ruined Scottish castles. Works were carried out at Edinburgh, Stirling, Perth and Roxburgh and also at Bothwell, Kinclaven, Cupar and Dunbar. However, if Edward hoped such defences would prevent the Bruce party's recovery he reckoned without Andrew Murray. Murray assumed leadership of King David's cause in 1335 and quickly marched to relieve his wife, the king's aunt, who was besieged in Kildrummy Castle by David earl of Atholl. During the next three years, Murray waged a relentless war on

Dunstaffnage Castle was sited by its MacDougall lords with similar strategic intentions to those behind Inverlochy, Rothesay and Urquhart. However, built as it was on a rocky outcrop without projecting towers and gatehouse, it was very different to those castles. (Undiscovered Scotland)

Edward III's supporters and castles. Avoiding major towns, Murray besieged Lochindorb in 1336, forcing Edward III himself to ride to the rescue of its defender, Atholl's beautiful, widowed countess. The next year, with Edward back home, Murray stormed the castles at Dunottar, Kinclaven, St Andrews and finally his own castle of Bothwell, leaving all in ruins after the practice of Good King Robert. Murray's strategy punched holes in Edward's defensive network, and though he died in 1338, his lieutenants were able to turn on the major garrisons. The English counter-attack stalled in an attempt to recapture Dunbar Castle from its redoubtable countess, Black Agnes Randolph. The fall of Perth in 1339, Edinburgh in 1341, Roxburgh in 1342 and Lochmaben in 1343 rapidly reversed Edward's advances. Though the defeat and capture of King David Bruce at Neville's Cross in 1346 saw Caerlaverock, Lochmaben and Roxburgh return to English control, these were border posts, not bases for the conquest of Scotland.

Lords and garrisons

The course of the Scottish wars repeatedly showed the importance of castles in the achievement of military and political goals. Whatever the pre-war functions of royal and baronial castles, these buildings possessed a strength and significance as strongholds in a period of warfare. This is clear with regard to great royal castles like Stirling, which commanded the best and lowest crossing over the River Forth, but also applied to many private houses. For example, Caerlaverock lay near the crossings by land and sea from Cumbria into Scotland, and westwards into Galloway. Bothwell in Clydesdale and Lochmaben in Annandale similarly sat near major north–south routes. Other castles, like Dunbar and Kildrummy, combined their locations near roadways with established significance as centres of local units of government. If rival kings sought control over provinces like Mar and the Dunbar earldom, the obvious means was through control of the chief castle, usually the caput or chief place of the region.

As well as physical location, the part played by baronial castles in these conflicts was also dictated by the loyalties and actions of their lords. For example, the earls of Dunbar were responsible for the defence of their castle. Although the countess defied her husband and held out against Edward I in 1296, the earls remained on the English side, albeit half-heartedly, largely

Stirling Castle on its rock. Though the buildings at this royal castle largely date from after 1500, the strength of the site is clearly evident, and the series of sieges and battles waged for control of Stirling clearly point to this too. (Undiscovered Scotland)

due to the location of their castle and lands. In 1314 Dunbar Castle secured Edward II's escape after Bannockburn, but the earl then promptly surrendered himself and his stronghold to King Robert. The earl changed loyalties again in the 1330s and, with Edward III's permission, rebuilt Dunbar, which Bruce had demolished. His further change of loyalty left Dunbar Castle as a dangerous base for Edward's enemies in Lothian. To avoid such problems the English kings could give castles and associated lands to English lords. In 1301, as he prepared to besiege the castle, Edward I gave Bothwell to Aymer Valence earl of Pembroke. Valence took custody of Bothwell and used it as his base while he served as Edward's lieutenant in Scotland. However, there was a danger that an English lord might not guard his castle with sufficient men. In 1311 Edward II installed his own captain and garrison in Bothwell because he worried that the castle might fall to the enemy, especially as he had quarrelled with Valence in England. A safer, but more expensive, option was to take a private castle into royal control. The strategically important castle of Lochmaben, the property of Robert Bruce's father, was held from 1298 by royal officials. This was despite the elder Bruce's loyalty to Edward I and indicates the value assigned to the safe custody of Lochmaben. The attack launched by Robert on Lochmaben in August 1299 may reflect a personal grievance about the status of the castle. Similarly the attacks of the young James Douglas on Douglas Castle in 1307, Robert Stewart's capture of Rothesay and Dunoon in 1334 and Andrew Murray's destruction of Bothwell in 1338 all show lords seeking to win back their own castles from the English.

Unlike Wales, where he constructed a chain of massive castles, Edward I and his successors sought to rule in Scotland through the existing castles built by the crown and nobility. This was a matter of necessity, based on the costs of fighting the Scots and wider financial problems, and a reflection of the value of these 13th-century buildings. Work was carried out in the English king's name in a number of places. Most intriguingly, in 1303 the architect of Edward I's Welsh masterpieces, James of Saint George, was paid for works. As the king had recently been at Kildrummy it has been suggested that the final form of the gatehouse there was the work in question. However, as the castle was held by Robert Bruce (at that time loyal to Edward), it is unlikely that large sums were spent by the king at Kildrummy. More extensive works were carried out by Edward III, who sought to rebuild castles demolished, wholly or partly, by Bruce. That baronial castles like Bothwell, Lochmaben,

Caerlaverock, Dunottar and Dunbar were made defensible, as well as the main royal castles, suggests considerable amounts of work. The results of this are hard to discern due to damage and later rebuilding, but throughout the period English works in Scotland seem to be more practical than stylish. A good example is provided by Lochmaben. Here Edward I took over the small Bruce castle by the loch in late 1298. In late 1299 orders were issued for the creation of a strong enclosure outside the castle guarded by a palisade, which was built by a force of 60 carpenters and workmen. This was the 'pele', a large encampment protected by earth and timber works that could house larger forces and supplies en route to other garrisons. Similar works have been identified at the royal manor of Linlithgow, between Edinburgh and Stirling, another strategically important site. Though unsophisticated by the standards of the previous half-century, these peles were cheap and quick to erect in time of war and strong enough to resist Scottish attack.

The strength and value of castles and peles depended on the men housed within them. It is hard to uncover much about the composition of Scottish garrisons, but the garrisons maintained by the English king were the front line of his rule in Scotland. Even at their height, the total number of men in these castles amounted to only a few thousand. The largest forces were in fortified towns. Berwick in the 1290s housed up to 1,200 men, while Edward III housed a small army in Perth after 1336. The garrison of Edinburgh in 1336 included 68 mounted men-at-arms, 71 hobelars (light horsemen) and mounted archers and numerous masons and carpenters. In 1313 Lochmaben

The great twin-towered gatehouse at Caerlaverock. The castle was heavily damaged by Edward I's siege of 1300 and was later partially demolished by Robert Bruce to prevent its use by the enemy. It was refortified in the 1330s and held by the English on and off until 1356. Its captor, the local knight Roger Kirkpatrick, was murdered in the castle by his treacherous guest, Sir James Lindsay, in 1358.

Buittle Castle in Galloway under archaeological investigation. Examination of the site has revealed evidence suggesting that castle was destroyed in the intense fighting in Galloway after 1332. Buittle certainly no longer acted as a major lordly residence after that date.

Castle and Pele were defended by 12 men-at-arms, 65 archers and 26 crossbowmen while a year earlier Bothwell was held by its Scottish captain, Walter fitz Gilbert, with 28 men-at-arms and 30 foot archers. It can be assumed that the mounted men-at-arms were fully armoured, and barded horses were specified at Lochmaben in 1299. Archers and crossbowmen were probably equipped with quilted armour. The origins of these troops were decidedly mixed. In Edinburgh in 1336, where the constable was a Scot, John Stirling, over half of the men at arms were Scots, while all the archers were English and there were five German mercenary knights. At Lochmaben in 1313 the leading knights were Roger Kirkpatrick, Thomas Torthorwald and William Herries, all local landowners and former tenants of the Bruces.

The roles played by these garrisons in English efforts to conquer Scotland were numerous. The constable appointed to hold castles often also had duties to run the surrounding sheriffdom or lordship. The garrison would assist in this, allowing the constable to raise rents and supplies from local estates, and to hold courts to determine local criminal and land cases. The command to William Felton, constable of Roxburgh in 1338, 'to pursue, arrest, capture and imprison in our castle all enemies against our peace and allegiance' stresses the link drawn by the English government between lawbreaking and armed resistance to Edward III's officials and indicates the use of castles as prisons. In a similar way, castles also functioned as depots for supplies and cash being sent into Scotland. Lochmaben, for example, acted as a post in a chain that stretched back to Annan and Carlisle and extended north into Clydesdale. Small in number though they seem, castle troops also acted as independent forces. By the 1330s English garrisons contained many mounted soldiers and used them in aggressive warfare. In 1336 the constable of Edinburgh, John Stirling, took 40 men-at-arms and 80 mounted archers from his garrison across the Firth of Forth in 32 small boats (each manned by seven sailors). Stirling then led his men 32 kilometres through Fife to confront a Scottish force under the earls of Fife, Dunbar and Sutherland besieging Cupar Castle. The earls fled, abandoning their siege engines and stores. The war could devolve into fights between rival garrisons and local forces. In 1299 the Scottish garrison of Caerlaverock harried the force in Lochmaben Castle and Pele in daily skirmishes until their captain, Robert Cunningham, was killed and his head stuck on Lochmaben's great tower. Lochmaben also came under attack from its lord's heir, Robert Bruce, who assaulted the castle for over three weeks in August 1299. The vulnerability of the castle led many of the English garrison to desert. To strengthen his position Edward I brought an army into the south-west and besieged Caerlaverock in June 1300. Even after the castle fell, Lochmaben was still at risk. In 1301, a Scottish army of 240 men-at-arms and 7,000 foot soldiers burned the town and attacked the pele on two days before withdrawing.

Even outside such periods of unusually intense warfare, the needs of garrisons dictated much English activity. Soldiers in castles required food and wages and this created problems of finance and of supply chains. In 1338, the isolated outpost at Cupar with a garrison of probably fewer than a hundred required 100 quarts of wheat, 120 of barley and 300 of oats, along with 30 casks of wine and 40 quarts of salt as about two months' supplies. This would require a supply convoy from either Perth or from the coast, crossing hostile ground and therefore needing an armed escort. The same applied to money. In May 1307 Robert Bruce's first victory was against a cavalry force under Aymer Valence at Loudon Hill. Valence was escorting the English treasurer and the silver being sent to pay garrisons at Ayr, Cumnock and Bothwell, which Bruce was trying (unsuccessfully) to seize. Failure to receive their pay pushed the troops at Berwick to mutiny in 1301 and created similar dissatisfaction at Lochmaben where many soldiers deserted.

Siege warfare

The importance of castles in maintaining military and political control made their capture vital. The Scottish Wars witnessed the full range of contemporary siege techniques, but a clear contrast developed between the approaches adopted by the two sides. Edward I was the master of conventional siege warfare. He relied on experts, engines and his extensive resources of manpower and money and demonstrated his thorough approach to war in a series of set-piece sieges. The first of these was laid against Caerlaverock where the garrison of 60 men had disrupted Edward's hold on the western approaches to Scotland. The preparations for this began in August 1299 with the construction of engines, but it was not until late June 1300 that Edward assembled a force of some 3,000 men and the campaign began. It was commemorated in a poem written by a clerk in the English army. This listed Caerlaverock's strengths:

A plan of Lochmaben Pele and Castle. In 1298 the large outer ward was created within a ditch and the bank topped by a pele or palisade. This cut off the loch-side promontory and increased the number of men who could be housed in the small castle. (John Richards)

> Its shape was like a shield … with a tower on each corner, but one of them was a double one, so high, long and large that under it was the gate … it had good walls and ditches filled with water.

With the sea and the River Nith to south and west, Edward set his camp to the east. Attempts were made to storm the castle and undermine the walls, but when these failed, the English settled down to a siege. Great stone-throwing engines were brought by sea and across country from Lochmaben. Under the expert, Brother Robert of Ulm, one small engine was assembled and threw for a whole day while 'three other engines of greater power and destruction' were set up. These engines 'crushed and cleaved whatever they struck' and under their bombardment the garrison quickly lost its nerve and sued for terms.

The three engines at Caerlaverock were almost certainly trebuchets, engines that relied on a counterweight which was winched down and then released to swing a beam and hurl a projectile. Missiles of 33 pounds have been thrown over 180 metres by such machines and they were objects of

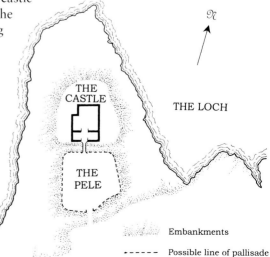

THE CASTLE

THE LOCH

THE PELE

Embankments

- - - - - Possible line of pallisade

power and fascination in the years around 1300. Many of Edward's engines bore names like *Segrave*, *Vernay*, the *Robinet* and, most famously, *Lupus Guerrae* or 'the War Wolf', the great trebuchet set up for the siege of Stirling in 1304. Their value meant that, once constructed, they were carefully stored. Seven engines were kept at Berwick in 1304, while others were at Dunbar and Inverkip. Locating engines in strategic, coastal depots also reflected the difficulty of moving and storing them. It took a week to bring an engine some 16 kilometres from Lochmaben to Caerlaverock, while no cart could be found that was big enough to carry the frame of 'the great engine' from Inverkip to Stirling.

A year after the capture of Caerlaverock, Edward led an army of nearly 7,000 men up the Tweed Valley and into Clydesdale. To clear his advance the king besieged Bothwell in September 1301. The great tower built by William Murray had probably been extended first by the English and then the Scots with a ditch and palisade. Some engines were carried by river to the siege, but these may only have been light bolt-shooting ballistas, of the type sent to Edward in October. The main weapon deployed against Bothwell was called *le berefray*. This was a belfray, or siege tower, which was wheeled against the wall and provided a fighting platform on the same height as the defenders and cover for archery. Edward's belfray was built in sections at Glasgow, loaded onto 30 carts and brought to Bothwell. Its approach to the walls was then prepared by a team of diggers and carpenters who built a timber roadway. In the face of this threat the garrison gave in before the end of the month. Edward's greatest siege was the climax of the first war at Stirling in 1304. After blockading the castle for five months, Edward slowly assembled his engines and, when isolation and fear led the garrison to surrender, the king made the Scots remain in Stirling to suffer bombardment. It was a mark of both Edward's harshness and of his pride in his siege methods.

The remorseless skill of Edward's experts probably convinced Robert Bruce (who served the English king at Stirling) to avoid such set pieces in future and to demolish rather than defend castles. This policy reduced the frequency of English sieges after 1306, but the war of the 1330s saw several highly significant clashes. In 1334 John Stirling, later constable of Edinburgh, besieged the castle of Lochleven. This castle was a simple stone enclosure on an island in the loch, and Stirling, having first built a base on the shore near Kinross, then tried to raise the water level and flood the castle by damming the outflow. Whether this was a realistic plan is doubtful, but when a Scottish sally broke the dam and flooded the English camp the enemy withdrew. A longer and more decisive siege occurred at Dunbar in 1338. The defection of the earl made Dunbar Castle a threat to English authority in Lothian. This was already challenged by bands of local knights, based in the hills to the south or in fortified caves. To remove the threat, Edward III sent an army under the earls of Salisbury and Arundel. In January 1338 they laid siege to the coastal stronghold. Two Genoese galleys were hired to cut off

A reconstruction of a counterweight trebuchet at Caerlaverock. The wooden box was filled with earth or lead weights. The beam was winched back and a missile placed in a sling on the end of the beam. When the beam was released it swung upwards, hurling the missile with massive force sufficient to breach a castle wall.

The castles in the Scottish Wars (1296–1357)

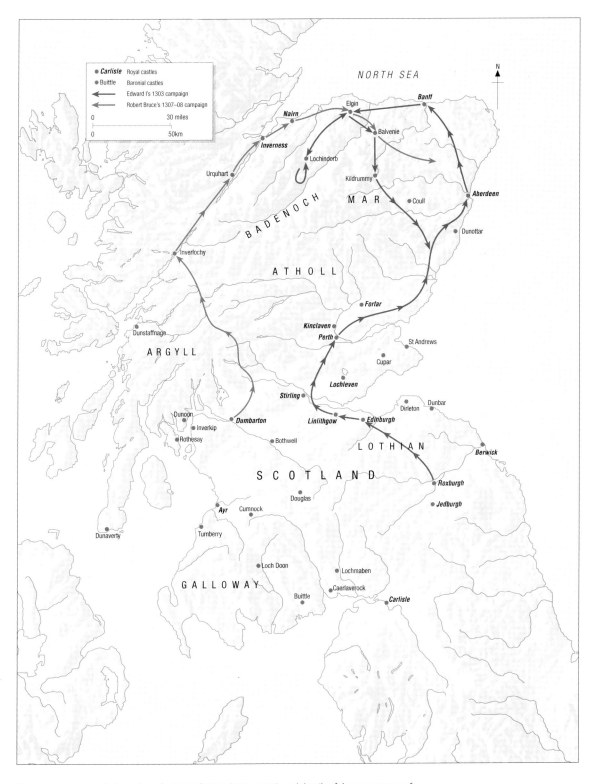

The castles that played a key role in the Scottish Wars (1296–1357), and details of the movements of Edward I in 1303 and Robert the Bruce in 1307–08.

The small island castle of Lochleven was one of the few castles holding out for the Bruces in 1334 when it was besieged. Later its lords, junior members of the Douglas family, built a tower house as their preferred residence.

the castle by sea, a 'somercastell' or tower for archers was constructed and engines hurled stones at the land walls. An energetic defence was maintained by the countess of Dunbar, 'Black Agnes', while Salisbury was probably hampered by the limited approach to the castle on land. He built a sow, a defensive screen on wheels, and sent men forward under it to undermine the wall. The countess halted this by using an engine inside the castle to drop a stone onto the sow, crushing it and those underneath. The castle was supplied from the sea by boats which slipped into Dunbar harbour by night and the besiegers were harried by local bands and sallies from the garrison. After an attempt to take the castle by treachery failed, Salisbury was recalled and the English withdrew in June.

Scottish siege methods were tailored by restrictions of resources and expertise. They did possess some engines, though probably fewer and smaller than Edward I's. Andrew Murray used one machine, named *Bostour* and probably a trebuchet, to great effect. Fear of the engine caused several small castles to surrender and it may have been deployed against Murray's own castle of Bothwell in 1337. Robert Bruce also had several engines, using them against Berwick and Carlisle without great success. At Carlisle in 1315 Bruce even constructed a siege tower, but unlike Edward I he did not prepare the approach and the tower bogged down and was destroyed by a sally. In general, however, the Scots relied on more 'low-tech' approaches. When Edward I failed to campaign in Scotland in 1299, his opponents were able to blockade key garrisons. Stirling surrendered to local barons after a long siege and Bothwell was hemmed in for a year and nine weeks until its warden gave in to 'famine and assault'. Blockade invited the English to mount a relief and caused problems of supply for the Scots too. Quicker results could be achieved by direct assault. In 1301 a large Scottish force sought to rush the palisade of Lochmaben Pele, but even against limited defences this attempt to storm failed.

Instead, when he faced up to a hostile network of royal and baronial castles held against him, Robert Bruce developed approaches that played to his forces' strengths. Rather than formal siege or assault, Robert and his captains used surprise and subterfuge. The classic method was the escalade, a sudden assault by ladders designed to catch garrisons off guard. At Roxburgh Castle in 1314, James Douglas chose the feast night of Shrove Tuesday, cloaked his men in black to evade detection by sentries and had them crawl to the walls like cattle. To scale the walls they used specially designed rope ladders with metal hooks at the top. These could be lifted and hooked over the rampart with a spear. Douglas and his men scaled the wall, killed the sentries and then overran the castle. The key to this tactic was the sudden, secret approach of the attackers. Garrisons were vulnerable when off guard. In 1341 Edinburgh was taken by a band of soldiers disguised as merchants and carters bringing supplies. These attackers blocked the gates with a wagon, allowing their comrades to rush the entrance. Contacts with the castle troops were also exploited. The high proportion of Scots in English garrisons provided opportunities for betrayal. Current or former garrison soldiers assisted the capture of Edinburgh in 1314 and 1341 and Berwick in 1318 and, after Bannockburn, Bothwell was surrendered by its captain who invited Robert to capture the refugee lords within his tower. Reliance on lightly equipped but mobile bands, on local contacts and on two generations of brave and crafty leaders proved more effective for the Scots than the English king's massive accumulations of manpower and medieval military technology. By 1357 only in the deep south, at Berwick, Roxburgh, Jedburgh and Lochmaben, did the English king hold Scottish castles.

THE CASTLES REBUILT, 1350–1450

The great castles

Though the long war with England continued until late in the 15th century, from the late 1350s it was a struggle of border invasions and long truces. The years of major conflict were over, but they left Scotland's castles in ruins. Of the great baronial residences, we have evidence of destruction at Bothwell, whose donjon was half torn down, at Caerlaverock, where the gate towers, the walls and the angle towers were all left only as stumps by the 1350s, and at Dirleton, where two of the towers were demolished. Literary or archaeological evidence similarly reveals damage or destruction at the castles of Balvenie, Kildrummy and Castlehill of Strachan in the north, Buittle and Cruggleton in Galloway, Dundonald in Ayrshire and St Andrews in Fife. However, as the threat posed by the English king's garrisons faded in the 1340s and 1350s, Scotland's nobles once again sought to construct buildings that were both defensible and settings for a lordly household and following. In the decades from 1350 to 1420 a new wave of castle-building produced reconstructed houses across the kingdom. The greatest of these were the work of the winners in the recent wars. The noble houses of Stewart and Douglas had upheld the Bruce cause and had risen to hold earldoms and lordships in many parts of Scotland. Magnates from these families built to display and cement their leadership of whole provinces.

Probably the first and, arguably, the best expression of this can be found at Tantallon in East Lothian, a few miles from Dunbar and Dirleton. It was here, on a cliff top overlooking the Firth of Forth, that William first earl of Douglas built a massive castle. This centred on a promontory site that could only be approached across a neck of land from the west. Douglas had this defended by the construction of a huge curtain wall of red sandstone, 15 metres high and nearly four metres thick. The thickness of the wall allowed chambers to be built within it. Towers were built at each end of the curtain wall and a mid-tower contained the gate into the inner courtyard. This mid-tower was constructed on a 15-metre-square plan and must have stood some 20–25 metres high, containing five storeys. The gate was protected by small projecting turrets and, slightly later, the defences were strengthened by the construction of a barbican. This twin-towered outer gatehouse acted as a further line of defence for the weak point in the wall.

The castle at St Andrews was first recorded in the late 12th century, but it was thoroughly destroyed in the wars of the 1300s and 1330s. It was rebuilt in the late 1380s as a courtyard castle on a rocky promontory. It served the bishops and later archbishops of St Andrews as a fortified palace close to the great cathedral.

The mid-tower was probably the residence of the constable. The lord's chambers were in the western tower, called the 'Douglas's tour'. This was largely destroyed in the 17th century and only a vague sense of its size and structure can be ascertained. However, a six-storeyed tower 15 or so metres in diameter would have formed a visually impressive and physically strong lodging for the earl. The Douglas tower stood adjacent to and opened into the castle's great hall. This hall was about 17 metres long and was built over the servant's hall, which was at ground level. Overall, Tantallon combines simplicity with complexity. It is essentially a great promontory fort with major defences only on one side. On the other three the cliffs provide the principal safeguard. The stonework of the castle is rough and uneven by comparison with the square-cut ashlar blocks of 13th-century buildings. The reliance on a great curtain wall suggests an attitude to defence that was built on crude strength. However the great residential towers, gate defences and halls indicate that Tantallon was built for a large and well-organized household. The earl, his family, constable and other servants probably had their allotted place in the halls and chambers while, beyond the wall, inside an earthen bank, a castle toun of wooden buildings could have housed a small army of retainers and hangers on.

Though it has been seen as the last of the curtain-walled castles of the previous century, Tantallon's layout and pretensions link it to its contemporaries after 1350. A few years later, William Douglas's cousin, rival and ultimate heir

⬛E THE REBUILDING OF ST ANDREWS CASTLE, c. 1390

St Andrews Castle was largely destroyed in the 1330s and was left in ruins until the last years of the century. Whilst it was derelict, a small tannery (1) stood on the land to the west. When Bishop Walter Trail rebuilt the castle in about 1390 he turned it

into a palatial residence for his household. The tannery (and its accompanying stench) was moved further off. Here the walls are shown largely complete, but work is still underway on the towers at the front (2, 3 and 4).

The rebuilding of St Andrews Castle, c. 1390

began work on his own castle. Archibald Douglas, variously known as the Grim, the Terrible or 'Blak Archibald', was the son of Bruce's lieutenant, the Good Sir James. In 1362 Archibald acquired the ruins of Bothwell Castle by marriage to Joanna Murray. During the next half-century, Archibald and his son rebuilt the castle. The result was very different to the plans of the Murrays in the 1270s. The Douglas castle was built in two clear phases. The first was pragmatic. Archibald constructed a wall which supported and defended the ruins of the great donjon and built a rectangular enclosure, much smaller than the one intended by the Murrays. There is no evidence that this enclosure was guarded by towers or gatehouse and the impression is given that Archibald's concern was to construct a defensible residence quickly and without sophistication. This aim may reflect the uncertainty of Douglas's position. In 1363 Earl William Douglas rebelled against King David II and may have attacked his cousin's lands at Bothwell. During the revolt, Archibald served the king and was later famed for having in his following 'a large company of knights and brave men'. The rebuilt castle at Bothwell would have served as a base for this retinue, presumably housed in wooden halls.

The simple structure built in the 1360s did not match the status of Archibald's line in the 1400s. In 1389 Archibald the Grim had inherited the earldom of Douglas and at his death in 1400 he bequeathed a vast connection of lands and followers to his son, Earl Archibald II. This earl was a man whose military and political ambitions matched his giant build. He would win a French duchy for his efforts, before dying in battle with the English. The works he ordered at Bothwell reflected his tastes and resources and may have been overseen by a French mason, John Morrow. Within the walls built by his father, Archibald constructed a gatehouse (now wholly destroyed), the impressive south-east tower and two ranges of domestic buildings. Along the east wall the earl had a chapel and hall built from high-quality ashlar blocks that contrast with the rubble-built work of the 1360s. The hall is about 25 metres long and lit by a row of finely made windows facing the courtyard. It was an impressive and comfortable setting for a great lord and, as at Tantallon, the earl's private apartments opened directly into the hall. At Bothwell, the earl lived in a great square tower house, which only survives in early drawings but which dominated the castle. The tower was entered through its own gateway into the hall, guarded by a small drawbridge. As well as allowing the tower to be defended as a last resort, this gate must also have served as an impressive entrance for those given access to the earl. Bothwell was well guarded, but many of its features were those of a palace as much as a fortress.

The rebuilding of the castles at Dundonald, St Andrews and Caerlaverock during the later 14th century also produced castle residences with extended and comfortable lodgings for lords and households. These designs may have owed something to the lessons of warfare that had shown that even the strongest castles defended by gatehouses and round towers were vulnerable to siege. The main concern in such buildings was for domestic accommodation, which, though defensible, was built for the lords, their family and servants. Perhaps the best example of such concerns is provided by Doune Castle. Eight miles west of Stirling, overlooking the River Teith, Doune was built between the 1360s and 1380s for Robert Stewart, second son of King Robert II. Stewart was earl of Fife and Menteith and later duke of Albany and effectively headed the royal government for most of the period from 1388 until he died in 1420. Like Bothwell and Tantallon, Doune was the fortified residence of a great noble. Like them too, the castle was superficially simple but contained a complex arrangement of rooms. Its circuit of walls lacked towers on both the south-west and south-east corners. All the main buildings stood along the north side of the courtyard. The core of the castle was the great tower, which stood above the gate and was connected by a hall block to a smaller tower residence containing the kitchens and other chambers. The great tower contained a lord's hall, outer chamber, chapel and a number of smaller chambers and closets or private rooms. The number of varied sizes of these apartments reflects a growing concern with privacy and levels of access to Duke Robert by his many servants.

Robert may have planned to construct other lodgings, a stable and a chapel round the other sides of the courtyard and make Doune one of his chief houses. Robert probably abandoned this plan when he was made hereditary keeper of Stirling Castle in 1372. Custody of this great royal castle relegated Doune to the status of a secondary residence, though the duke and his family stayed there regularly until the 1420s. By making the centrepiece of his new castle a tower lodging, Robert Stewart was adopting the same approach to castle-building as the Douglas magnates and King David II, who had built a tower house, known as David's Tower, as the main accommodation in the rebuilt Edinburgh Castle in the 1360s. These towers were all constructed as elements in larger castles with a curtained-wall enclosure and other towers and domestic buildings. However, several Douglas lords also built major residences that were dominated by free-standing towers. These were all in areas still affected by warfare, such as the stark tower of Hermitage in the wild moors of Liddesdale or Newark Castle, a large tower house, built by Archibald II earl of Douglas in the early 1420s as his family's residence in Ettrick Forest. However, the best example of this type is provided by Threave. This castle was built on an island in the River Dee in Galloway in the years after Archibald the Grim was made lord of this unstable frontier province. Archibald needed a secure base for his followers in their lord's efforts to 'cast down the captains', and force the submission of the 'wild men' of Galloway.

The eastern curtain wall at Bothwell shows the fine south-eastern tower and the foundations of the tower house built by Archibald II earl of Douglas in the early 15th century.

The hall of the Black Douglas castle at Bothwell and, to the right (adjoining the south-east tower), the castle chapel makes clear the aspirations of the family for a princely residence.

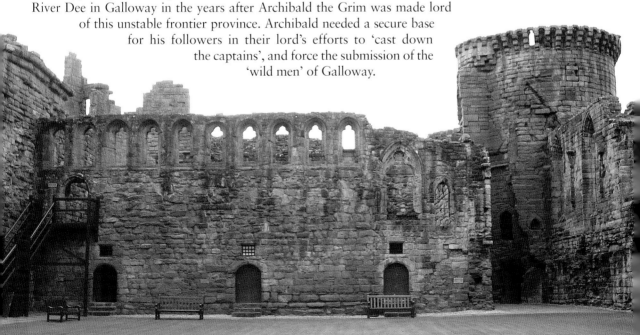

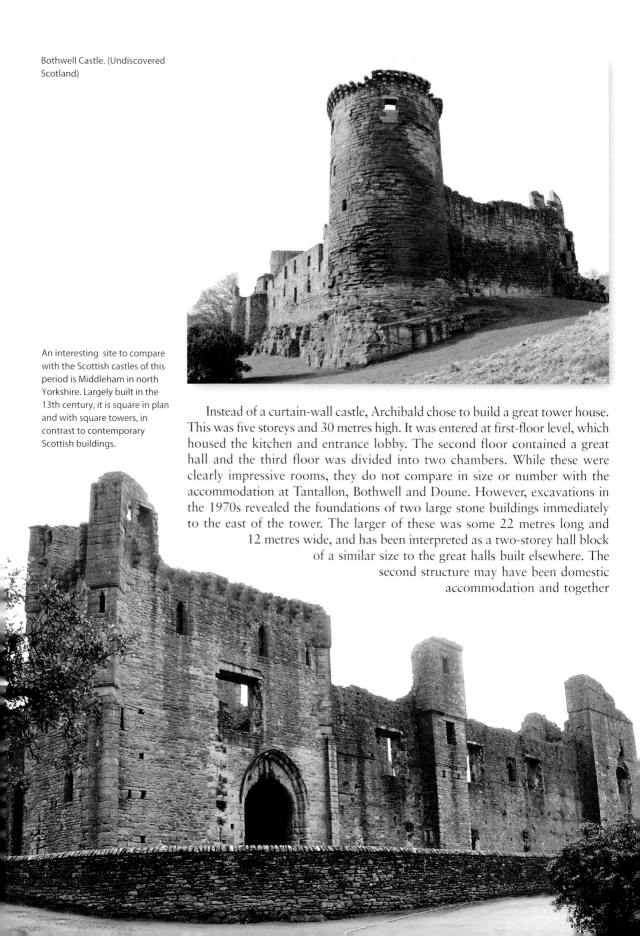

Bothwell Castle. (Undiscovered Scotland)

An interesting site to compare with the Scottish castles of this period is Middleham in north Yorkshire. Largely built in the 13th century, it is square in plan and with square towers, in contrast to contemporary Scottish buildings.

Instead of a curtain-wall castle, Archibald chose to build a great tower house. This was five storeys and 30 metres high. It was entered at first-floor level, which housed the kitchen and entrance lobby. The second floor contained a great hall and the third floor was divided into two chambers. While these were clearly impressive rooms, they do not compare in size or number with the accommodation at Tantallon, Bothwell and Doune. However, excavations in the 1970s revealed the foundations of two large stone buildings immediately to the east of the tower. The larger of these was some 22 metres long and 12 metres wide, and has been interpreted as a two-storey hall block of a similar size to the great halls built elsewhere. The second structure may have been domestic accommodation and together

these stone halls could have housed the large household of Archibald the Grim and his heirs. There can be no doubting the importance of Threave. Archibald himself died in the castle in 1400 and his heirs clearly regarded it as their principal house in the south-west. Though it lacked the walls traditionally associated with castles, Threave had military functions. Its island location gave it a degree of security, but it was for use as a base from which Douglas retainers could ride out against their enemies that persuaded Archibald to build his castle there. The tower house at Threave provided a defensible core to the castle, which could be guarded by a small garrison. In the early 1450s, when the Douglas earls were facing conflict with King James II, they strengthened the site by knocking down the stone halls and building a low wall round the three landward sides of the tower. This wall was angled to deflect artillery shot and had three towers. Wall and towers were equipped with gun loops for handguns and culverins (small cannon). With this fortification, Threave was able to withstand a royal siege in May and June 1455, only surrendering in early July when, with no relief force in the offing, the captain allowed himself to be bought off with a pardon, a job and gold.

The ruins of the two-storey hall block at Tantallon. Behind it loom the broken remains of the great Douglas Tower. Before its destruction in 1651 this had been the main residential feature of the castle complex.

However, the popularity of the tower house was based on wider considerations. Large tower houses of four to six storeys high were visually impressive, inside and out, and allowed for division into halls and smaller chambers. While Tantallon, in particular, but also Bothwell and Doune, look more like curtain-wall castles, they were also designed for magnates, who were the heads of households, and retinues, which could

swell to the size of small armies. For such lords (and ladies), castles were barracks, camps, and places of council and court on a scale not required by nobles in the previous century. These functions produced buildings that were less architecturally satisfying but convey an impression of rugged strength and personal ambition that captures the era in which they were built.

The smaller castles

In contrast to the 13th century, the greatest castles of the years 1350 to 1450 were the work of the chief nobles of the kingdom. However, castle-building was not limited to these Douglas and Stewart magnates. The period also witnessed the construction of a large group of smaller castles, the work of the ranks below the earls. This largely undifferentiated class of barons ranged from powerful lords with estates scattered through many parts of Scotland and considerable influence in local politics and in the king's councils to a local laird with rights of justice covering a single parish. Before 1300 it would have been the norm for most of this group to build and reside in hall houses of timber and stone, some surrounded by ditches but many unfortified. In the century from 1350 a new style would become the definitive core of the Scottish noble residence. As we have seen, the tower house had been incorporated into the great halls and ranges of major royal and magnate castle-building, but it was to dominate the form of lesser structures even more clearly. There are examples of small residences being adapted to incorporate this new feature.

At Lochleven the small island castle had an imposing five-storey rectangular tower house built into the north wall of the older enclosure. This work may date to the reign of David II in the 1360s, making the tower at Lochleven an example of the style, perhaps modelled

Hermitage Castle, seen here from the north-west, evolved from a manor house to a strong tower and finally, with the addition of two substantial wings *c.* 1400, a forbidding and massive fortress in the border lands of Liddesdale. (Undiscovered Scotland)

The main approach to Doune Castle confronted the visitor with a frontage that was clearly well fortified, but which lacked the integrated defences of earlier castles. It had no flanking round towers and well-defended curtain-wall heads, such as those found at Caerlaverock and Kildrummy.

on David's Tower at Edinburgh. A different approach was adopted nearby at Aberdour. Here a 13th-century hall house was heightened into a tower with a strange, slightly off-true rectangular plan. Though it collapsed in the 19th century, the decision to transform hall into tower is revealing of tastes in the later 14th century.

The popularity of tower residences, which usually stood between four and seven storeys in height and like Lochleven and Aberdour were normally of rectangular plan, was the result of a number of factors. The first of these was probably the resources of the builder. As at all periods, some lesser noble lineages gained greater incomes from land and pensions through inheritance, marriage and promotion, but the relative peace experienced after the great wars and the opportunities of rewards from service to crown and great lords probably boosted the disposable revenues of a wider group. In the late 14th century, barons like Thomas Hay of Yester and John Crichton of that ilk clearly possessed the wealth to build tower houses. Hay's castle overlooking the Tweed at Neidpath near Peebles was a substantial and impressive residence, while Crichton's tower was a smaller building, but still marked a greater expense than a hall house.

At Doune Castle the extensive kitchens were located in a second tower house that abutted the great hall. Also in this tower were additional chambers for servants and guests. At Threave the separate stone halls may have played a similar role.

Questions of resources can be linked to the issue of family aspiration. The Crichtons and Hays of Yester were amongst a larger group of families seeking increased status in the years after 1350. As before 1300, castle-building could be a product of newly acquired land and rank. The minor border family of Pringle received the lands of Smailholm from the earls of Douglas in 1408 and after the fall of their lords in 1455 became direct tenants of the crown. These events marked the advance of the family and

Tower houses and halls – Doune Castle in the late 14th century

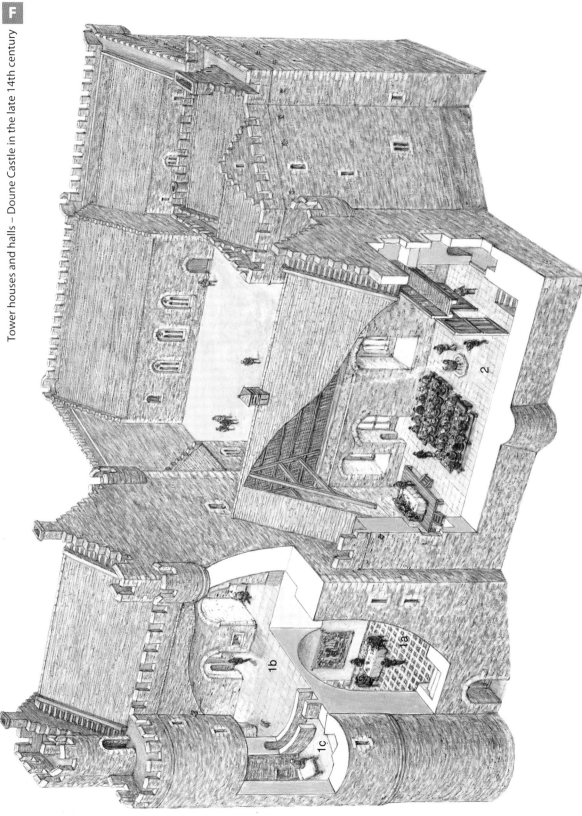

Newark Castle. The lands between the upper Tweed and the waters of Ettrick and Yarrow in the middle Borders had originally been a great, royal hunting forest. In the 14th century they became a private lordship of the Douglas earls. In about 1420 the earls built this substantial tower as their main residence there.

encouraged them to build their tower at Smailholm. Though relatively small, this tower perched on a crag was a mark of status visible for miles around. The Pringles built a hall and kitchen block around a small courtyard, but these buildings were probably no more than those found at many manor places. It was the tower that was the castellated part of the house, built to command the landscape and display the local lordship of its owner. Though strategic sites also relate to security, the choice of crag sites for Crichton, Neidpath and Craigmillar near Edinburgh, and rocky promontories on the narrows of the Forth for the mid-15th-century towers at Rosyth and Blackness, show similar concern for displayed rank from the barons who built these castles. To own a castle was to claim higher standing amongst one's peers. The years from 1424 produced a run of 'licences to crenellate', letters from the king that gave permission for a noble to build a castle. The men who sought these were concerned not just to avoid offending the irascible kings of these decades. They were all minor barons seeking a written statement of their right to a castle. The licence given by James I to James Dundas allowed him to construct 'the tower or fortalice [small fortified house] of Dundas in the manner of a castle with walls and ditches for the which and fortified after the manner of the Scottish kingdom'.

Such towers could be small and simple structures. Smailholm was a four-storeyed building about 10 metres by 15 metres in ground plan, containing a small hall and two chambers. Craigmillar, which was built for the minor baronial family of Preston in the early 15th century, showed the possibilities for greater development. To the rectangular tower which contained hall and

F   TOWER HOUSES AND HALLS – DOUNE CASTLE IN THE LATE 14TH CENTURY

The arrangement of the main rooms at Doune has led some to see it as a castle built by an insecure lord, who sought to separate himself and his family from his hired retainers and retain personal control of the main gate. Such a separation would have been impossible. Instead the design shows concern for comfort and levels of access to the lord. The gate tower would have served as the residence for the lord, his family and immediate household with its own main hall (1a) and upper hall (1b), with a separate chapel and chambers in the side tower (1c). The great hall (2) would have been used for the larger retinue, but also for courts and larger festivities.

With its unusual shape and stonework, Neidpath is a striking early tower house. Its slightly off-parallel plan was dictated by its narrow site.

chamber was added a single wing making an L-shape. The wing housed the stairs and kitchen creating a more spacious and better-served house. By the 1430s and 1440s complex and sophisticated residences were being constructed within the tower house by lesser barons. William Lord Borthwick received his licence to crenellate in 1430. He built Borthwick Castle south of Edinburgh as both a massive and impressive fortified house and a highly developed lodging. To the main block were attached two wings making a C-shape. With seven floors this tower contained considerable space. While the central tower housed a double-height great hall, an inner hall, and chapel, the wings contained a kitchen, chambers for officials, withdrawing chambers for the lord and his family and a series of private rooms. Five separate stairs linked different parts of the tower, less for security than to allow varied levels of access for servants and family. However, other barons chose to develop their castles on more traditional lines. Sir William Crichton rose far in royal service, becoming chancellor of Scotland in 1439. He chose to demonstrate this new importance by turning his family's tower house into a courtyard castle with a great hall and domestic ranges built in a square. Crichton, who secured earldoms for his son and cousin, aspired to magnate status and may have built to match Doune and Bothwell rather than Borthwick just across the valley.

Amidst these signs of rising aspirations and fortunes it is easy to underestimate issues of security as an influence on these smaller castles. Though the period of major conflict with England was in the past, fears of war or political

Smailholm Tower in the middle Borders is a fine example of the type of residence built by lesser nobles in the marchlands towards England. The concentration of tower houses in this region was clearly linked to the prevalence of feud and raid, but Smailholm also provided a comfortable residence.

violence were still very real. During the 1380s, 1400s and 1450s there were sustained periods of warfare with England and, even during formal truces between the kingdoms, the Borders operated as a military zone witnessing raiding and reiving by English garrisons and by the lesser nobles and kindreds of the marches. The building of Smailholm by the Pringles, of nearby Cessford by the Kerrs and even of Neidpath by the Hays, provided strongholds for defence and bases for raiding

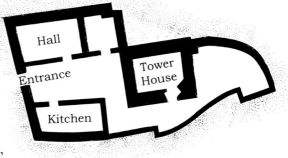

Excavations at Smailholm have revealed that the tower was not a stark, isolated and primitive structure. Beside the tower, within a walled courtyard, there were ancillary buildings. (John Richards)

in this unsettled zone. In times of open war, the crown expected lords to man and defend their own towers as part of the defence of the realm. Similar concerns applied in the north where growing concern with the raiding of Highland caterans led to a statute being passed in 1427 that ordered all lords with lands in the region in which 'in aulde tymes thare was castellis, fortalycis and maner places', to repair them and provide for their defence. This would encourage the 'gude polising' of the country, an indication that castles retained a clear role as defensive structures in local disturbances.

Individual barons may have shared such anxieties. Castles like Borthwick, Crichton, Dundas, Rosyth, Blackness and Craigmillar may have been built in a period of relative order and lay in the heartlands of Scotland in Fife and Lothian, but their owners still needed strong houses. During the minority of James II in the 1440s all of these tower houses may have acted as refuges and bases. In West Lothian the proximity of Blackness and the Crichtons' fortified house at Barnton to the Douglas castle at Abercorn led to a local conflict in 1443 in which Barnton was captured by a 'great host' led by the young king and Earl William Douglas. Two years later Rosyth and other towers must have served as refuges during the 'herschip [harrying] of Fife' by Douglas's allies and in 1449 King James and Douglas besieged and took Dundas castle. The civil wars of the early 1450s between king and Black Douglas witnessed a series of sieges, the most important of which were those of the now-demolished castle of Abercorn and of Threave in 1455. At Abercorn, the king's guns proved decisive, bringing down towers and walls and their slow approach may have helped persuade the garrison of Threave to surrender (though bribery also played a part). While against such weapons the tower houses of barons and lairds might seem puny, in the more normal violence of raid and feud they retained a value as secure houses, garrison points and refuges.

CASTLE LIFE IN LATE MEDIEVAL SCOTLAND

Threave, October 1426

To convey a sense of what it was like to live in a castle in early 15th-century Scotland it is necessary to draw on individual pieces of evidence from chronicles and poems, from family papers and royal records, from the ruined remains of the castles themselves and from structures and artefacts uncovered by archaeological work. Pulling such varied and scattered information together to create a coherent picture is a difficult task and it can be helpful to employ a single occasion in a specific place and at a specific time to give a focus to what we know. Choosing Threave in October 1426 allows us to look at a site which has been thoroughly examined by archaeologists and at a castle held by the Black Douglas family, a dynasty which produced plentiful evidence of its interests and activities.

Threave Castle. The image of the gaunt, massive tower alone on its island is misleading. Between the 1370s and 1450s the tower lay at the centre of a cluster of buildings and was a residence of one of the richest families in Scotland. (Undiscovered Scotland)

Threave Castle in 1426 was unusual in two ways. Firstly, it acted as a permanent residence for a major noble household. Most castles owned by great lords were only visited occasionally by their proprietors. Secondly, it was in the possession of a woman. The lady of Threave was Margaret Stewart, dowager Duchess of Touraine and Countess of Douglas and elder sister of the king, James I. Like all noble widows, Margaret was entitled to a share of her husband's lands and in May 1426 the king had confirmed her as the lady of Galloway. Ownership of this great lordship, which stretched from Dumfries to the Firth of Clyde and was worth over £500 in rents, made Margaret a wealthy woman in her own right. She had lived in Galloway before the death of her husband and younger son in battle in France in 1424 and chose to make Threave her home from 1426 until her death in 1449. Margaret's affection for the province and her pious concerns were suggested by gifts to local religious houses and for the construction of a new bridge over the River Nith at Dumfries. When she died, Margaret was buried in a magnificent tomb at Lincluden Priory on the outskirts of Dumfries.

Margaret was far from unique as the lady of a castle. A generation earlier, her namesake, Margaret countess of Angus, had dwelt in the great cliff-top castle of Tantallon. She secured it as her residence after the death of her lover William earl of Douglas in 1384 and in 1388 held on to it despite pressure from many of the kingdom's leading nobles. Within its walls the countess raised her son by William, George Douglas, and, after his death, her grandson. Similarly, after being arrested at Doune Castle in 1425, witnessing the trial and executions of husband, father and sons by James I and spending 12 years in the king's custody at Stirling, Isabella duchess of Albany was released and allowed to live in the island castle of Inchmurrin on Loch Lomond. Inchmurrin had belonged to Isabella's father, the earl of Lennox and in this, now wholly ruined, castle, the duchess gathered her half-brothers and grandsons and presided over a household until her death in 1456.

There is no evidence about the size and organization of Duchess Margaret's household. Noble dowagers in late medieval England of similar rank employed

G THREAVE CASTLE IN OCTOBER 1426

This illustration shows the entrance of Archibald earl of Douglas into the inner courtyard at Threave Castle in October 1426. The earl and his entourage (1) are being met by his mother Duchess Margaret, her ladies and her male servants (2). The Bishop of Galloway (3) is also in attendance. The arms of the earl can be seen on his banner (4). The tower house is to the right (5), with the great stone hall blocks (6 and 7) in the foreground.

5

2

3

1

4

6

7

51

between 40 and 60 servants who would receive a regular fee for their duties and resided in the castle. Only a few of these would have been women. The duchess would have had a group of personal attendants, ladies of the chamber, who might well have been recruited from the daughters and sisters of her noble tenants and retainers. Beyond these most of those in attendance would have been male. The names of only the most important officials and councillors can be traced. Margaret's chief official was her chancellor, John McGillhauch, a cleric who held the duchess's seal, by which her letters were authenticated, ran her staff of clerks and headed her council. Alongside the chancellor was Alexander Mure, a lesser nobleman and cousin of Margaret who was her steward. This post made Mure head of the daily running of the household, responsible for discipline and duties amongst the servants. Mure combined this office with the post of bailie of Kirkcudbright, the area of eastern Galloway in which Threave lay. As bailie he would have collected rents and renders of oatmeal for the duchess and may also have held her court in this part of the lordship. Below these chief officials would have been a wider group of clerks with different duties and squires who acted as gentle attendants, as guards and as messengers for the duchess. They served for payment of a regular fee but also in the hope that they would receive greater rewards from their wealthy employer. One servant, Margaret's 'beloved squire', Andrew Agnew, was made keeper of Lochnaw Castle soon after the duchess took control of Galloway. In 1427, the chancellor, John McGillhauch, protested that, having promised to give him the valuable provostship of Lincluden Priory, the duchess was being persuaded to give it to another household clerk, Gilbert Park. Park 'remained near the duchess' to secure her patronage, but McGillhauch 'by persevering with the duchess', finally obtained the promotion. Servants were not simply employees, they were men on the make, who by showing their efficiency or other talents sought to win the rewards which could be bestowed by the lord or lady. The tower house and its adjacent halls would have been the setting for these efforts.

In October 1426 this household was preparing for a major occasion. Threave was to house a meeting of nobles and churchmen from across the south-west, including the Bishop of Galloway. The most important guest was to be Duchess Margaret's son, Archibald III earl of Douglas. As the first meeting between mother and son since Margaret had been confirmed as Lady of Galloway, there was business to be discussed. Like many nobles, Douglas may have resented the way his own inheritance had been impoverished to support his mother, especially as Margaret had involved her brother, the king, in Douglas family affairs. The earl was at Threave by 26 October. He had probably reached the castle from the east, perhaps coming from Lochmaben Castle in his lordship of Annandale 38 kilometres away. He could easily have made this journey with his own entourage in one day's travel, but may have lodged at Dumfries, Lincluden or even Caerlaverock on his way. His train of attendants was probably suitable for such a great lord. It included not just his own close servants like his secretary, John Railston, but noble tenants and friends including Herbert Maxwell lord of Caerlaverock Castle and the earl's steward of Annandale. Lesser barons

Borthwick Castle. (From MacGibbon and Ross, *The Castellated and Domestic Architecture of Scotland*, 1887)

would have brought their own servants, making the progress of mounted men and their foot servants, carts and pack animals an impressive sight as it approached the ford over the River Dee to the north of Threave.

Unlike his mother, the earl and his household were used to such journeying. As a great lord with major estates in Clydesdale, Dumfriesshire, and through the Borders and Lothian who was required to attend the royal court and parliament, Archibald was frequently on the road. The records show that, during the previous year, the earl had spent time in lodgings at Edinburgh and Perth, in his lordship of Lauderdale and in the castles he owned at Bothwell, Newark and Lochmaben. The wide responsibilities of the earl meant that he resided irregularly in these castles. During his absence major castles like Bothwell and Lochmaben stood largely empty and the duties of keeping them secure and ready for use as houses and strongholds were delegated to keepers. These men were often lesser nobles from the immediate neighbourhood. For example, Earl Archibald employed his local tenant, John Turnbull, as keeper of Newark Castle, and the neighbouring lords of Symington were hereditary constables of Douglas Castle. At Lochmaben the 'keeper, captain and governor' for life was a lesser servant of the family, Michael Ramsay. Ramsay undertook to 'kepe the castell' on his lord's behalf in peace and war against all others and was rewarded with rents worth £80 per year collected from the earl's estates in the district and rights to the fishing of Annan Water. In conjunction with this post, Ramsay also acted as chancellor and chamberlain of Annandale, holding the earl's courts and collecting his rents. There were concerns for lords that by giving custody of castles to lesser men, they risked losing control of them. Grants of custody to keepers often included a clause that gave the lord free access to the castle at any time with as many men as he wished. Such fears were real. Earl Archibald's father had been forced to besiege Edinburgh Castle when he was its custodian after a dispute with his deputy in the stronghold. When a lord like Douglas resided in one of his castles it was probably a major occasion. As well as his personal household and local officials, the earl was often attended by a gathering of local knights and lesser tenants, anxious for his favour and support.

Though Threave Castle was used to the presence of its lady, the prospect of Douglas's arrival with his entourage must have required major preparations. These preparations would have occupied the whole of Threave Island. As discussed previously, Threave was not the classic enclosure castle but a great tower house with stone halls and timber buildings constructed around it. The timber buildings that stood north of the castle mostly housed the craftsmen who served the needs of the household. The numerous artefacts found at the site indicate that these craftsmen included leatherworkers, smiths who worked in lead and iron and wood turners. The latter produced numerous bowls, one of which has been discovered, stamped with the 'bludy heart' badge of the

The extent to which a simple tower house could be expanded is shown by Crichton Castle. Chancellor William Crichton built this massive residential range alongside his family's tower. William moved his lodging to the second tower at the left of the picture. The result was like a small version of the royal palace at Linlithgow.

Douglas family. Other buildings would have acted as stables, barns and slaughterhouses as well as the accommodation for the families of the duchess's household servants. At Kildrummy and Tantallon similar collections of wooden-framed houses existed beyond the curtain wall. The arrival of the earl of Douglas, the Bishop of Galloway and other barons in late October 1426 would have required the gathering of livestock, dried fish and meal in this castle toun. It would also have required the accommodation of many additional men. The tower house would only have housed the most important guests, perhaps the bishop and the earl with their personal attendants in the chambers on the upper floors. Other lords might have been lodged in the separate hall block or the other stone range which stood east of the tower, but many of their followers would have been squeezed into the houses of the castle toun.

Though this was an exceptional occasion, the design of Threave suggests that servants tended to be lodged, in the old fashioned manner, in public rooms like the great hall. The tower house built in the 1430s at Borthwick, by comparison, contained many separate chambers and wall closets, which were probably intended to give private lodgings to different members of family and household. In English houses, like Caistor Castle and Bolton Castle, such small chambers were assigned to specific household members or to visitors and their furnishings recorded in inventories. There are no comparable inventories of 14th- and 15th-century Scottish castles. Some indication of the possessions of Duchess Margaret at Threave can be gleaned from the archaeological evidence of the site and by reference to the near contemporary will of Margaret's kinsman, James Douglas lord of Dalkeith. As well as a poorly executed seal matrix, for imprinting the duchess's arms on documents, which bore her arms, a gilded locket or relic case and a gilt cross probably decorated with pearls were found at the site. As a wealthy dowager Margaret would have owned many luxury items. Douglas of Dalkeith's will listed dishes, basins and spoons of silver, rich robes made of cloth of gold, embroidered fabric and waxed leather, some of them imported from Flanders, and books of law, grammar, romance and religious practice.

It would have been surprising if a pious and wealthy princess like Margaret did not possess a small library, including bibles and books of worship. The will also included many pieces of jewellery. Some of these had religious significance, like the hair of Mary Magdalen enclosed in a gilded silver case, or the cross that included a piece of 'the cross on which Jesus hung'. Others had a medical function, like the sapphire set in gold 'which cures the blood'. Most numerous were rings of gold set with jewels. One of these was bequeathed to the Black Douglas family. It had a ruby and was inscribed with the words '*Vertu ne pus avoir conterpois*' and may have been amongst Margaret's possessions.

Duchess Margaret's own wealth in books, plate, clothing and jewels would not have been kept hidden. For a major occasion, like her son's visit, they would have been on display, the books and plate perhaps in a specially constructed closet called a buffet. While the visit of the earl and bishop to Threave in 1426 must have had a major impact on the normal routine of household life at the castle, the daily timetable would probably have retained its basic pattern. English evidence makes clear that, even in the households of noble men and women, the daily schedule was structured around religious observation. The kitchen servants would have risen at five to put food out for the rest of the household. The gates would be opened at six in the winter and the household officials would celebrate mass before the lady arose at seven. She, too, would attend mass and matins in her chamber before breaking her fast with her guests. During the morning the officials carried out their financial duties while the lady might attend high mass in the chapel in the tower house or spend time at leisure with her guests and servants. Lunch probably took place in different locations and at different times with the lady dining at 12 o'clock in the hall in the tower and her servants eating earlier, perhaps in the outer hall block. The afternoon was again free and may have been the time for formal meetings between the duchess and her guests. The evidence for the whole gathering comes from a charter, a formal confirmation of property rights made by the duchess to a kinsman, Sir William Douglas of Lesswalt. Earl Archibald gave his formal consent for his mother's charter and the bishop and other barons acted as witnesses to the document. The castle was a natural location for such legal and political business, just as it was for the social gathering of kin, tenants and neighbours. The afternoon concluded with evensong at four. Supper was then at five or six o'clock. After the meal was the time for entertainments, for music to be played or sung or for stories to be told, like those of the earl's great-grandfather, Sir James Douglas, Robert Bruce's heroic lieutenant, which have survived in various forms. At about eight o'clock the lady and her guests would retire, perhaps hearing prayers in their chambers. After this the gates and doors of the tower and halls would be locked.

The tomb of Archibald III earl of Douglas at St Bride's Kirk, Douglas. The son of Duchess Margaret was one of the leading lords of Scotland. He had led armies in France and at his death in 1439 was lieutenant-general of Scotland for the young James II. Margaret's own tomb is at Lincluden Priory near Dumfries.

The castles and tower houses of late medieval Scotland were not only, or even primarily, military strongholds. For all its stark appearance and border location, Threave was a living residence during its heyday. Though built as a place of power, designed to defend and dominate eastern Galloway, its normal life when it was an aristocratic centre was less martial. Margaret duchess of Touraine and lady of Galloway presided over a domestic, not a military, establishment. The century from 1350 to 1450 was a period of continued war and occasional political upheaval, but almost all castles were the same. Their use and design were dictated by the daily tastes and needs of house and household, lord and lady.

THE AFTERMATH: BARONIAL CASTLES c. 1450–1700

It is easy to see the decline of the castle as beginning in the mid-15th century, linked to the coming of gunpowder artillery and changes in aristocratic values and political structures. However, while there is some truth in this, most of the castles we have looked at continued to have value as defensible houses for another two centuries. The importance of these castles as centres did depend on the fate of their owners. The fall of the dukes of Albany in 1425 meant Doune became a minor royal hunting lodge before passing to various hereditary keepers. The forfeiture of the Black Douglas earls saw Threave, Bothwell and other castles cease to act as the principal houses of great magnates. Threave, for example, became the responsibility of local royal officials in the west march towards England.

The fall of the Black Douglases in 1455 also witnessed the first effective use of artillery in an internal Scottish conflict, when King James II attacked Abercorn and Threave. The capture of these castles did not make stone towers and curtain walls obsolete in war. The massive curtain wall of Tantallon withstood two royal sieges in 1491 and 1528. The guns of James IV and James V proved unable to make a breach. Tantallon was strengthened in the 1520s by the construction of new works, a stone barbican in front of the foretower and a fortified entrance to the outer ward. As at Threave, these works were designed to house artillery and were copied in other adapted castles. At Dunbar and St Andrews, squat stone artillery blockhouses were sited to defend the older walls behind, while the border tower at Cessford was given earthwork defences which served well against a major English attack in 1523. Even without such additions simple tower houses like Smailholm and Hermitage remained places of refuge in the warfare with England during the 1540s. Unless the enemy brought cannon against a tower, it preserved a defensive value.

Similarly there was no clear break in the tastes of Scotland's elite. The tower house remained the favoured style of construction for nobles in the century after 1450 and there was clearly no sense that the front presented by older castles was archaic and out of date. Instead adaptation took the form of spacious new halls, apartments and tower houses inside the earlier walls. Kildrummy, Dirleton and Urquhart all had new tower residences constructed by their owners in the early 16th century. At Caerlaverock, the 13th-century façade was rebuilt after the wars and added to with extensive interior works in the 15th and 16th centuries. In 1634 the impressive east and south ranges, known as the Nithsdale Lodgings, were built. Though these reflected modern styles and requirements, the Maxwells were happy to adapt rather than supplant their ancestral home. The same was true of the Gordons at Huntly, where from the late 16th century a palace block provided a lavish expression of the family's status directly alongside the late medieval tower house and earlier motte. On a smaller scale the Prestons enveloped their tower at Craigmillar with extensive domestic ranges and ancillary buildings. The tower was converted into storerooms and kept as the great hall, but the flanking buildings housed the family apartments. Similar adaptations can be found at Crichton and the small Aberdeenshire castle of Tolquhoun.

With these alterations many medieval castles remained in regular use into the 17th century. Kildrummy provided the Erskine family as earls of

The buffet at Dirleton Castle. This decorated wall recess at one end of the great hall block, which was added to the castle in about 1500, was designed to display the wealth of the lord in plate, religious items and books to his guests.

Mar with their principal residence until the end of that century, Craigmillar was the Prestons' main house until the mid-18th century and Huntly and Caerlaverock were still dwelt in by the Gordon and Maxwell families until the mid-17th century. Tantallon was regarded by the Red Douglases as their strongest place of residence in the 1590s. Behind this longevity of use were considerations of economy and fears about security, but also the desire of great, noble houses to preserve their connections to ancestral houses. These places of strength with their walls and towers conveyed an image of martial power, which still appealed to their owners in a later age.

It was the decades after 1640 that marked the real demise of the Scottish medieval castle. This change was the result of the periods of war and peace during the later 17th and early 18th centuries. The civil wars of the 1640s and 1650s and the Jacobite conflicts of 1689–90, 1715 and 1745 saw many castles used in military roles once again. Such roles came at a price in terms of damage and destruction. In 1640 the Maxwells' support of Charles I led to the sieges of Caerlaverock and Threave by the Covenanter opponents of the king. Both resisted for 13 weeks before surrendering. Their continued strength in warfare sealed their fates. They were deliberately slighted, their walls breached and their roofs removed to prevent further use and they rapidly became ruinous. Mighty Tantallon suffered a similar fate. Used by the Scots as a base for attacks on Cromwell's advancing army in 1651, the castle was finally pounded into submission by a bombardment from 16 large guns, which brought down the end towers. From then on Tantallon ceased to be used as a major residence. Service in the Jacobite Wars similarly led to the ruin of Kildrummy, Huntly and Doune.

Alongside the ravages of war, these medieval buildings also fell out of fashion as houses of the nobility. This shift is clearly demonstrated at Bothwell where the Red Douglases chose to abandon the castle in favour of a new mansion house in the modern style, which was built to the east. This stately residence proclaimed the peaceful, civilian virtues now valued by the aristocracy. The tower house that was the residential core of Bothwell Castle was torn down to provide stone for the new mansion. Following the Restoration of 1660 and

Aberdour Castle in west Fife showing the collapsed remains of the tower house. The end of the 16th-century range that extended from it and became the core of the new mansion at the site is also shown.

the Union of 1707 many other noble families made similar choices, abandoning or demolishing ancient seats in favour of houses in the new style. The medieval castles were left to decay until the revival of interest for the Scottish past a century later.

VISITING THE SITES

Aberdour Castle, Fife (Historic Scotland)
In Aberdour, 13 kilometres east of the Forth Bridges on the A921 and adjacent to Aberdour railway station. A 13th-century hall house remodelled as a tower house and then a Renaissance mansion with terraced gardens.

Balvenie Castle, Moray (Historic Scotland)
In Dufftown (between Elgin and Huntly) on the A941. A 13th-century castle of enclosure, which was rebuilt in the 15th century.

Blackness Castle, West Lothian (Historic Scotland)
Six kilometres north-east of Linlithgow on the A803 and then B903. A 15th-century tower house on the shores of the Firth of Forth that was converted for use by artillery.

Bothwell Castle, South Lanarkshire (Historic Scotland)
At Uddingston south of Glasgow. Entrance signposted off B7071. The ruined donjon remains from the Murray's 13th-century castle. It is incorporated into the fine 14th- and 15th-century residence built by the earls of Douglas.

Caerlaverock Castle, Dumfries and Galloway (Historic Scotland)
Between Annan and Dumfries on the B725 (12 kilometres south of Dumfries). The ruins of the famous triangular castle with its double-towered gatehouse and later ranges.

Coull Castle, Aberdeenshire (private, but ruins can be viewed from exterior)
Four kilometres north of Aboyne on the B9094. The ruins can be reached along a track that starts by Coull church and runs south.

Coulter Motte, South Lanarkshire (Historic Scotland)
On A73 road between Biggar and Lanark, 2.5 kilometres south-west of Biggar. A small motte dating from the later 12th century.

Craigmillar Castle, Edinburgh (Historic Scotland)
Four kilometres south of Edinburgh city centre off the A7. An early 15th-century tower house enclosed by later ranges and walls.

Crichton Castle, Midlothian (Historic Scotland)
Twenty kilometres south-east of Edinburgh on the A68. Signposted on B6367 from Pathhead (four kilometres). A 14th-century tower house that was expanded into an impressive courtyard castle in the mid-15th century.

Dirleton Castle, East Lothian (Historic Scotland)
In Dirleton on the A198 between Gullane and North Berwick (five kilometres west of North Berwick). Set in extensive gardens, this is a fine, compact, domestic castle with works from the 13th, 15th and early 16th centuries.

Doune Castle, Stirling (Historic Scotland)
In the village of Doune, 16 kilometres north-west of Stirling by the A84. A grand courtyard castle built *c.* 1360s and 1370s with imposing tower house residence and great hall.

Dundonald Castle, South Ayrshire (Historic Scotland)
Twenty kilometres from Ayr and eight kilometres from Kilmarnock off the B730. A fine tower house on the summit of a hill built on the site of an earlier stone enclosure castle.

Hermitage Castle, Borders (Historic Scotland)
Off the B6399 between Hawick and Newcastleton (eight kilometres north of Newcastleton). A stark and unusual border keep in the wilds of Liddesdale. Built to command this route into Scotland in the 14th century.

The small but attractive castle at Tolquhoun in Aberdeenshire shows the way in which lesser nobles developed their residences in the 16th century. On the left stands the old tower house (built *c.* 1420), which was incorporated into the martial front that was constructed for show in the 1580s. The gatehouse and round tower are merely for display, and behind them lies a stylish and comfortable Renaissance mansion.

Inverlochy Castle, Highland (Historic Scotland)
Three kilometres north-east of Fort William off the A82. The ruins of a square curtain walled enclosure with four round corner towers dating from the later 13th century.

Kildrummy Castle, Aberdeenshire (Historic Scotland)
Sixteen kilometres west of Alford on the A97. Though considerably ruined, Kildrummy is still one of the finest medieval castles in a magnificent setting in the hills of Mar.

Lochleven Castle, Perth and Kinross (Historic Scotland)
Located on an island in Loch Leven. In the summer it can be reached by boat from Kinross. A stone enclosure with a 14th-century tower house built into the walls.

Lochmaben Castle, Dumfries and Galloway (Historic Scotland)
Off the B7020 south of Lochmaben. The intriguing ruins of a castle, which was fortified by the English with a pele.

Morton Castle, Dumfries and Galloway (Historic Scotland)
Off the A702 between Carronbridge and Crawford (just over a kilometre from Carronbridge). A hall house of the 13th century in a remote location.

Neidpath Castle, Borders (private, but open to public)
On the A72 1.5 kilometres west of Peebles. An early tower house with an unusual rhomboid plan.

Newark Castle, Borders (private, but exterior can be viewed)
Off the A708, 6.5 kilometres west of Selkirk at Broad Meadows. Visible on the south side of Yarrow Water.

Peel of Lumphanan, Aberdeenshire (Historic Scotland)
Off the A980 at Lumphanan, 14.5 kilometres west of Banchory, 0.8 kilometres from the village. An imposing 13th-century earthwork.

Rothesay Castle, Argyll and Bute (Historic Scotland)
In Rothesay on the Isle of Bute. A circular enclosure probably built in the early 13th century with round towers added after 1230.

St Andrews Castle, Fife (Historic Scotland)
In the centre of St Andrews. Ruins of the bishop's castle on a cliff-top promontory. Though first built in the 12th century, the remains date from the later 14th and subsequent centuries.

Smailholm Tower, Borders (Historic Scotland)
Off the B6404 between Kelso and St Boswells (10 kilometres west of Kelso). A fine, small border tower of the 15th century standing on a crag and commanding the surrounding lands.

Tantallon Castle, East Lothian (Historic Scotland)
Five kilometres east of North Berwick off the A198. A massive red sandstone fortress on the cliffs overlooking the North Sea. The fortified residence of the

Red Douglas earls of Angus remains an impressive reminder of the power of Scotland's medieval lords.

Threave Castle, Dumfries and Galloway (Historic Scotland)
On an island in the River Dee. Reached by boat during the summer. The castle lies off the A75 five kilometres west of Castle Douglas. The imposing tower house built by the Black Douglases in the late 14th century provides the main surviving part of this castle.

Tolquhoun Castle, Aberdeenshire (Historic Scotland)
Between Old Meldrum and Ellon just off the A920 (10 kilometres from Ellon). A small tower house of the early 15th century, which later formed part of a fine renaissance castle.

Urquhart Castle, Highland (Historic Scotland)
On the A82 along the west shore of Loch Ness, 2.4 kilometres south of Drumnadrochit. Well known for its magnificent location, Urquhart was also a key noble stronghold in the Highlands.

BIBLIOGRAPHY

The series of guidebooks produced by Historic Scotland for the sites in their care provide excellent detailed discussions of the architecture and history of individual castles. They are available at the sites themselves and directly from Historic Scotland.

Brown, M. *The Black Douglases: War and Lordship in Late Medieval Scotland* (East Linton, 1998)
Calendar of Documents Relating to Scotland preserved in H.M. Public Record Office, ed. J. Bain and others, 5 volumes (London, 1881–88)
Coulson, C. *Castles in Medieval Society* (Oxford, 2003)
Cruden, S. *The Scottish Castle* (Edinburgh, 1960)
Dixon, P. 'Design in Castle-Building: The Control of Access to the Lord', *Château Gaillard* 18 (1998), pp 47–57
Duncan, A.A.M. *Scotland: The Making of the Kingdom* (Edinburgh, 1975)
—— 'The War of the Scots', *Transactions of the Royal Historical Society*, 1992, 6th series, ii (1992), pp. 125–51
Ewart, G. *Cruggleton Castle: Report of Excavations 1978–1981* (Dumfries, 1985)
Fawcett, R. *The Architectural History of Scotland: Scottish Architecture from the Accession of the Stewarts to the Reformation* (Edinburgh, 1994)
Good, G.L. and Tabraham, C.J. 'Excavations at Threave Castle, Galloway, 1974-8', *Medieval Archaeology*, 25 (1981), pp 90–140
Lewis, J. 'Excavations at Bothwell Castle, North Lanarkshire', *Proceedings of the Society of Antiquaries of Scotland*, 127 (1997)
Liddiard, R. *Castles in Context: Power, Symbolism and Landscape, 1066–1500* (Macclesfield, 2005)
MacGibbon, D. and Ross, T. *The Castellated and Domestic Architecture of Scotland from the Twelfth to the Eighteenth Century*, 5 volumes (1887–92)
McNeill, T. *Castles* (London, 1992)
Oram, R. 'Continuity, Adaptation and Integration: the Earls and Earldoms of Mar c. 1150–1300' in Boardman, S. and Ross, A. *The Exercise of Power in Medieval Scotland c. 1200–1500* (Dublin, 2003)

—— and Stell, G. (eds) *Lordship and Architecture in Medieval and Renaissance Scotland* (Edinburgh, 2005)

Prestwich, M. *Armies and Warfare in the Middle Ages: The English Experience* (Yale, 1996)

Registrum Honoris de Morton, 2 volumes (Edinburgh, 1837)

Simpson, W.D. 'The Architectural History of Huntly Castle', *Proceedings of the Society of Antiquaries of Scotland*, 56 (1921–22), pp. 134–63

—— 'A New Survey of Kildrummy Castle', *Proceedings of the Society of Antiquaries of Scotland*, 62 (1927–28), pp. 132–48

——''Bastard Feudalism' and the Later Castles', *Antiquaries Journal*, 26 (1946), pp. 145–71

—— 'Bothwell Castle Reconsidered', *Transactions of the Glasgow Archaeological Society*, (1947), pp 97–116

—— 'The 13th Century Castle of Dirleton', *Scottish Historical Review*, vol. 27 (1948), pp. 48–56

—— 'The Donjons of Conisborough and Bothwell', *Archaeologia Aeliana*, fourth series, 32 (1954), pp. 100–15

Stell, G. 'Late Medieval Defences in Scotland', in D.H. Caldwell, *Scottish Weapons and Fortifications, 1100–1800* (Edinburgh, 1981)

Tabraham, C. *Scotland's Castles* (Edinburgh, 1997)

—— 'Smailholm Tower: a Scottish Laird's Fortified Residence on the English Border', *Chateau Gaillard*, 13 (1987), pp. 227–38

Thompson, M.W. *The Decline of the Castle* (London, 1987)

Watson, F. *Under the Hammer, Edward I and Scotland* (East Linton, 1998)

—— 'The Expression of Power in a Medieval Kingdom: 13th-century Scottish Castles', in Foster, S., Macinnes, A. and MacInnes, R. (eds), *Scottish Power Centres* (Glasgow, 1998)

Woolgar, C.M. *The Great Household in Late Medieval England* (New Haven, 1999)

Wormald, J.M. *Lords and Men in Scotland: Bonds of Manrent* (Edinburgh, 1985)

Yeoman, P. *Medieval Scotland* (Edinburgh, 1995)

Caerlaverock Castle encapsulates the experience of Scotland's baronial castles of the high Middle Ages. Built in the 13th century, it was demolished in the wars of 1296 to 1356. Rebuilt in the later Middle Ages and then adapted with a Renaissance range in the 1630s, Caerlaverock's days as a residence were ended in 1640 when great breaches were blown in its south wall.

GLOSSARY

Ashlar	Cut stone blocks often used to face rubble-filled walls.
Bailey	Courtyard.
Ballista	A small siege engine that fired a large dart or bolt from a giant crossbow.
Barbican	An outer defence for a gateway.
Belfray	A wooden tower mounted on wheels or rollers designed to be pushed up against a castle wall as an archery platform or bridge onto the wall.
Blockhouse	A thick-walled tower built to house artillery.
Caput	'Head' place of a lordship where the lord held his main court.
Crenellation	Wall defence or battlement.
Curtain	The principal defensive wall of a castle.
Donjon	The great tower of a castle, usually the lord's residence and a defensive strongpoint.
Drum tower	Tower with a circular ground plan.
Enceinte	The castle enclosure.
Escalade	Surprise assault on a castle using ladders.
Forework	External defence for a gateway.
Fortalice	Small castle or tower.
Herschip	A plundering raid.
Hoarding	Wooden platform built out from the parapet to command base of the wall.
Laird	A minor nobleman.
Licence to crenellate	Permission to build a castle.
Loop	Opening in the wall to allow handguns to be fired by defenders.
Machicolation	Battlement brought forward to command base of the wall.
Magnate	A great lord.
Merlon	The protective blocks of a battlement.
Moat	Enclosing defensive ditch in front of or around a castle.
Motte	An artificial earth mound used as the base for a wooden hall or tower.
Mural chambers	Chambers within a wall.
Palisade	Defence constructed of timber stakes.
Parapet	Summit of a wall designed to protect the wall walk.
Pele	Enclosure defended by an earth bank and timber palisade.
Promontory fort	A castle that was constructed on a cliff top where only the landward front needed to be protected by walls.
Postern	Small gateway.
Rampart	Summit of a bank or wall.
Range	Residential block.
Sow	A wooden or wicker screen to protect attempts to undermine curtain walls.
Summer castle	A wooden fortification used as a defence for archers and engines in a siege.
Tower house	Fortified residence in the form of a four- to seven-storey tower.
Trebuchet	A stone-throwing engine powered by use of a counter weight.
Turret	A small tower.
Vault	Stone ceiling.
Wall walk	Walkway along the summit of the curtain wall for use by the garrison.
Ward	Courtyard.

INDEX

Figures in **bold** refer to illustrations